The Expanded Life

The Expanded Life

Myron S. Augsburger

ABINGDON PRESS, Nashville and New York

THE EXPANDED LIFE

Library of Congress Cataloging in Publication Data

AUGSBURGER, MYRON S. The expanded life. 1. Beatitudes. 2. Christian life—Mennonite authors. I. Title.
BT382.A9 226'.9'066 72-689

ISBN 0-687-12419-0

MANUFACTURED BY THE PARTHENON PRESS, AT NASHVILLE, TENNESSEE, UNITED STATES OF AMERICA

To the students at Eastern Mennonite College
who are both a stimulus and an inspiration in our
association as disciples

Foreword

The author of this book has been a personal friend and acquaintance for more than twenty years. It has been my privilege to be associated with him in two fields of Christian service—evangelism and Christian education both on college and seminary level.

To work with him in these various relationships has been a pleasant experience, and it is recognized by those who know him that he represents an unusual convergence of gifts and talents. He is an able preacher and teacher, an efficient administrator, lecturer, and prolific writer. This book is now added to the growing accumulation of works from his pen.

Many persons have undertaken to write about the Sermon on the Mount, but Dr. Augsburger's approach is new and different. I am unaware of any other work which approaches the Sermon on the Mount in this manner. It is original, creative, and stimulating. Dr. Augsburger has a high appreciation for his Anabaptist heritage which comes through with clarity and pungency. He is a literalist in his interpretation of the Sermon on the Mount with regard to the question of peace and nonresistance as held by the so-called peace churches.

Dr. Augsburger leaves no doubt about the fact that he believes in genuine New Testament conversion which will be expressed in a life of obedient discipleship.

This book is highly recommended to the reader with the assurance that it will be received with real interest and appreciation.

George R. Brunk, Dean
Eastern Mennonite Seminary

Preface

"No man knows Christ truly unless he follow him daily in life." Discipleship was interpreted in this manner by a sixteenth-century leader in the Free Church movement. This is my conviction as well, believing that in the Sermon on the Mount, Jesus is calling us to "disciple" all of life.

To add another work to the many written to interpret Jesus' sermon is my testimony to the significance of his message. In sharing these chapters I have followed an approach which to my knowledge has not appeared in other treatments. This fact itself may lay my approach open to question; however, seeing the Beatitudes as an outline for the sermon is meaningful for me. This perspective will, I am sure, be of value to the reader in study and devotion.

While I am not unaware of the critical questions relating to the several accounts of Jesus' sermon in Matthew and Luke, this work follows the content the Holy Spirit has given us through Matthew's writings. Further, recognizing that some dispensationalists pass over this sermon as not a part of the Word of God for the "Church Age," I would only affirm that Jesus' words are for all Christians in all times, a position supported by Luke's account, as well as by the confirmation of the Epistles. Believing in the inspiration of the Scriptures I do not hold the Gospels to be of higher authority than the Epistles, for the full interpretation of Christ can only be found when one reads passages such as Romans, Colossians, Hebrews, etc. In the Gospels we understand the man Jesus as seen in his words and deeds, thereby discovering his life-style. In this sermon we are confronted with "the Jesus way" of life.

In giving this work the title *The Expanded Life* the true nature of discipleship is emphasized—an enriched and broadened life, relating the principles of Christ to our total life pattern. Conversion to Christ prepares us to live!

Myron S. Augsburger

Contents

1

Behaving Our Beliefs

His disciples gathered around him, and he began to teach them. (Matthew 5:1-2)

The Sermon on the Mount has its own outline—the Beatitudes! Studying this Sermon of sermons I discovered that the Beatitudes form a series of themes which make up the sermon. Jesus presents the call to an expanded life, a life enriched by sharing his will. This is the life of a disciple, a life of obedience to the Master himself. Following this introductory chapter on discipleship, we will follow the pattern of projecting a beatitude into the sermon to see how Jesus himself interpreted its meaning. When I discovered this approach to the sermon it made the total message become more clear to me.

Jesus introduces us to a new idea of righteousness, one of right relation with himself and his quality of life rather than right relation to a system of laws. The law is good when observed in the right spirit, but it can take one no higher than the level of the law itself. It only points to the possibility of a new life. This life is described as experiencing "the righteousness of God," a discipled relationship with Christ.

A disciple is one who is disciplined to the attitudes and purposes of Christ. Discipleship is a demanding way of life. While a legalist is hard on others and easy on himself, a disciple is easy on others and hard on himself! To take up the cross and follow Christ is costly. This is not simply accepting the "sweet Jesus" of pietism, but it is obeying the exalted Lord of the Resurrection. Discipleship recognizes that the Kingdom of Christ is a current reality. We become members of that Kingdom now. With citizenship in the Kingdom of heaven, we become "global citizens," calling men and women of every nation and race to join hands as brothers in Christ. This association of disciples is transcultural, freeing the church from mere cultural religion and ethnic mentality.

In the New Testament, conversion is not moralistic but personalistic. We are not converting to a code but to a person—Jesus Christ. Conversion is a surrender, a yielding of one's self to the lordship of Christ. This is a change of direction at the very core of one's life. Once self-centered, one now becomes Christ-centered. Paul writes, "When anyone is joined to Christ he is a new being: the old is gone, the new has come" (II Corinthians 5:17).

We each need to experience this newness, rather than to excuse ourselves in sin.

The story is told of four boys who were late to school. When they finally arrived it was noon, and they offered the excuse of having had a flat tire. To their surprise the teacher was most understanding, commenting that this problem had happened to her already. Then she added that they had missed something that morning and they would need to take a little test. Asking the four boys to get pencil and paper and to take separate seats she said, "There is just one question to this test: which tire was flat?"

The test of reality is the authentic life. It can be said of Jesus, "nobody has ever talked the way this man does," because nobody ever lived the way this man lived. (John 7:46.) He was a whole person, with God in control of his life. He had close friends without becoming enslaved by his peers. He had a good education for his day without being pedantic. He enjoyed sexuality without needing sex. He was able to exercise leadership without exploiting people. He lived by love without becoming a "pushover." His eyes flashed fire about social injustice and religious bigotry, yet his anger with issues did not harm persons. "Nobody has ever talked the way this man does," because nobody ever lived the way this man lived!

Words are not the only means by which one speaks; the total life communicates. The Master shared God's Word by *what he said,* by *what he did,* and by *what he was.* If we honestly accept Christ we must accept the whole Christ, not only part of him. It is as we know him that we can hear him, for a man's approach to Christ affects his hearing of Christ's words. If we would hear correctly, we must hear what he is saying. There is a danger that while he speaks we may hear only what we put into his words.

To truly know God we must meet him through his acts in history. He has come to us in Jesus Christ. In Christ I have come to know God as a person of love and justice. My surrender to Christ was a conversion, a change of direction from living for self to living for God. This is an inner repentance, changing one's attitude toward God, toward one's self, and toward sin. Such a conversion involves discipleship, following the way of Christ.

The evidence that one has experienced conversion and knows the reality of regeneration is seen in the direction his life takes as a follower of Christ. Most significantly, the converted person now becomes a member of the Kingdom of Christ. Our citizenship is in heaven, or as Paul writes, He [God] rescued us from the power of darkness and brought us safe into the kingdom of his dear Son" (Colossians 1:13).

To be a Kingdom member means that we are disciples of Christ.

A disciple is one who identifies himself with a person and a persuasion. Jesus said, "Whoever declares [the King James Version reads "confesses"] publicly that he belongs to me, I will do the same for him before my Father in heaven" (Matthew 10:32). Confessing means that we are called to be activists for Christ! Too many confessing Christians are apathetic about the real issues of life and society. When other causes are more important than introducing people to God, we no longer truly know God. The Christian Church is guilty of apostasy when it elevates other things above Christ. Our calling is to let God be God in our lives. If one ceases to believe that this will make the basic difference in life, then the cause which he has put in place of God is his idol. A disciple dares to confess Christ in the face of all the movements of the world. He will not have god-values other than God himself.

The Master's words in this message deal with motives, with attitudes, as basic to our behavior. The message begins with a list of affirmations called beatitudes. The term is descriptive of the whole sermon, be-attitudes! Attitudes are at the heart of the matter, for the spirit with which one approaches life determines much of life's character. What happens within us is more important than what happens to us. We must first be free from ego-centeredness if we would live unselfishly. Or conversely, we develop a violent spirit before we demonstrate it by acts of violence. We suffer from our own insecurity, as a cause of our reacting to the threat of others. Long before the science of psychology was discussed as such, Jesus was dealing with the psychology of behavior.

This sermon is the greatest deeper-life message Jesus ever preached. Here the reasons for our behavior are laid bare. The greater question we face is not what we do, but why we do what we do. This is the basic issue of ethics.

In the stream of history God has bound himself to us.

From the moment he created man in his image everything changed for God—forever! He will always be dealing with us. As God shares himself with us he asks only that we share ourselves fully with him. This is a relation of understanding and love.

To make this a reality, God has unfolded through history a revelation of himself. This self-disclosure progressed through the Old Testament until "when the right time came, God sent his own Son" (Galatians 4:4). This is his full revelation—God has come to us in Christ.

A disciple is one who, meeting God in Christ, continues to learn from him. It is great to experience a basic commitment to Christ, but the test of our commitment, as in marriage, is in how we work it out in life following our entry into covenant. In Christ we learn fully what God is like. "For it was by God's own decision that the Son has in himself the full nature of God" (Colossians 1:19). Jesus Christ revealed God in his words, in his deeds, and in his character. Having dared to say, "Whoever has seen me has seen the Father," he added: "Whoever accepts my commandments and obeys them, he is the one who loves me" (John 14:9, 21).

The measure of our faith is revealed in whether we seek to know God by more adequately understanding Christ, or by our own philosophical speculation apart from Christ. Is it not strange that modern man, who believes so deeply in the greatness of man, stumbles over seeing God in the Son of man? Actually there is no greater affirmation of humanness than the Incarnation—God could identify as man.

**To be a Kingdom member
means that we share in God's grace and will.**

I have found sharing my life with God to be a demanding experience. There is so much in the ego that wants to be God, to try and live adequately before God by one's own power. But the more honest I became, the more it became clear that I need God to save me from myself. I need the Savior, today, for the same reason, to save me from being only myself. And God will do just that, come to us in grace, share himself with me!

Grace is God's graciousness, his willingness to involve himself with us. God not only has forgiving grace but transforming grace as well. Not only does God forgive our rebellion but he makes us new men. I have found this to be first an inner experience, before it becomes an external discipline.

True faith is not limited to participation in sacramental rites. It has about it the sense of faithfulness, of an existential participation with God. One who truly believes is able to say, "My Lord and my God." This confession marks the beginning of a new life. But when one's love is new, one's purpose is new, and one's motive is new. We participate with God rather than stand against him. Just as in a marriage of love there is a change from "I" and "mine" to "we" and "ours," so in faith one now practices a communion of unity with God.

God is at work in the world creating a people for himself. This is a new community made possible through Christ. As an individual I experience this community of God's new people as I give myself to him and to each of them. His call to discipleship is not an appendage to the work of salvation, it is the actualization of that salvation now in the stream of history. We are already God's people in spirit and character. We receive our directives and our spiritual dynamic from him. He is Lord of our lives and of the new community of believers.

When we accept Christ as Lord we accept him as Lord of history. The Incarnation is final—we do not go back behind Christ for further directives nor do we add to him. He is the full Word of God, about God and about true humanness. The test of my faith is in the question, "Is Jesus Christ my Lord? Can I let him be God in my life?" Only when I commit myself honestly to him can his Spirit do his work in my life.

To share the regenerating work of the Spirit is truly being "born again." This experience marks the beginning of new life, a life in direct, immediate relation to God. It means that I am doing business with God for myself. There is nothing second-hand about this. No one is handing me a ready-made religion; I am encountering a living Christ. The change this produces in my life is conceptual, but it is more than that. I am changed by God's Spirit to live by love, peace, and holiness. This is participation in the answer to the search for meaning. The degree in which I share my life with Christ is the degree to which I participate in wholeness.

To participate in God's Kingdom means living by his will. God's will for character is universal; it is the same for all of us—to be Christlike. But God's will for service is an individual matter, as I discover how God can use me to fulfill his purpose for mankind, where I am, and with the opportunities I have. To know God's will there are a few guidelines that I have found helpful. First, believe that God wants to lead you. Second, believe that he will put "interests" into your life. Third, believe that he will open doors for service and look for them. Fourth, pray over the options honestly—not all opportunities are equally good for you with your particular interests and gifts. Fifth, counsel with spiritual friends—take time to weigh the conviction; if it is of God's Spirit it won't be fleeting. Sixth, act in good faith, for God is more concerned about your attitude in a role than about your achievements. And seventh, remain sensitive to his corrections, for in decision-making God would rather adjust your course than have you remain immobilized by indecision.

To be a Kingdom member means that we live by Kingdom principles.

Many people have a problem relating faith and works because they have failed to experience a faith that works. The Bible speaks of faith which works by love. This emphasis relates obedience to my identification with Christ. Obedience is an expression of loyalty to him. Too many Christians have been afraid to emphasize obedience lest it appear that they are working for salvation. Behaving our beliefs does not permit us to separate faith and works; rather, we hold them together in a working faith.

The essence of the gospel is not good advice but good news—we can participate with God in life. This relationship is the saved life. Ethics and grace are not at odds. We can relate ethics to Christ, to Christology, in the same way that we relate salvation to Christ. We can behave in covenant relationship. Ethics for the believer becomes the guiding principles of the new life, a spiritual motivation for our behavior.

The Sermon on the Mount presents these principles for Christian behavior. The emphasis is not on a code of works but on a conviction of principles for decision-making. This sermon is a spiritual rather than a legalistic guide. It elevates attitudes above act, spirit above letter, principles above patterns. But it is not simply suggestive—Jesus means what he says about the character of life he is asking of his disciples. The New Testament makes clear that we are not under the law but under grace. But as D. Martyn Lloyd-Jones says, "That does not mean that we need not keep the law. We are not under the law in the sense that it condemns us; it no longer pronounces judgment or condemnation on us. No! but we are meant to live it, and we are even meant to go beyond it. The argument of the apostle Paul is that I should live, not as a man who is under the law, but as Christ's free man." [1]

The Sermon on the Mount makes us aware of our need for a new birth, for the transforming power of God's grace. We study this sermon with the words of Jesus in

[1] D. Martyn Lloyd-Jones, *Studies in the Sermon on the Mount* (Grand Rapids: Eerdmans, 1959), Vol. I, p. 12.

mind, "You can do nothing without me." (John 15:5.) As we study the sermon itself we will follow his be-attitudes as the outline for the message. This is his formula for happiness. This is an exciting guide to understanding the sermon. We will now examine how these beatitudes are projected into the sermon as an outline, and how Jesus' own interpretation expands them.

2

Happy Are the Spiritually Poor

Happy are those who know they are spiritually poor: the Kingdom of heaven belongs to them! (Matthew 5:3)

It takes a humble spirit to be enriched by others. Pride limits the growth of one's spirit; humility expands the spirit by learning and receiving. Jesus said, "Remember this! Unless you change and become like children, you will never enter the Kingdom of heaven" (Matthew 18:3). A child has the ability to trust, to receive. The ability to trust enables one to develop.

Humility is not negating or looking down on one's self. The experience of fellowship with God should give one a good self-image. Salvation gives one a great sense of personal worth. Humility is simply the ability to recognize the true nature of our worth under God, and then to use our gifts to enrich the lives of those whom we touch.

Jesus calls us to the path of humility, to take up the cross and follow him. We are to die to our selfish life so that we can be effective in our relation to others. Only when we know how to receive from God are we able to point others to his goodness. In contrast, arrogance and conceit rob us of many rich experiences in friendship and interchange with others.

The philosopher Nietzsche felt that Christianity was inadequate because of its emphasis on kindness, love, humility, meekness, and forgiveness. He advocated the achievement of the strong person in arrogance, power, initiative, and strength. He had an ardent disciple in Adolf Hitler, who said, "Love is weak, hate is strong; we'll use hate and we'll rule the world." But history reveals that they who take the sword perish with the sword, while those who live and die by love inherit the Kingdom of God.

This Kingdom is a literal reality but is spiritual in nature, just as the physical resurrection of Christ was a literal event but ultimately spiritual in character. Apparently the Jewish people of Jesus' day looked for a materialistic Kingdom and missed the meaning of the Kingdom which is coming in Christ. This Kingdom has come, is coming, and will yet come in a greater fulfillment. Of this Kingdom, Jesus said, "The Kingdom of God does not come in such a way as to be seen," and again, "The Kingdom of God is within you" (Luke 17:20, 21). We become participants in the Kingdom of God now. The Christian's primary citizenship is in heaven; even now

I am a member of Christ's Kingdom through his salvation.

Some persons who hold a dispensational view of the Scriptures see the Kingdom as the Jews did, and see it postponed to some future age. These persons regard the Sermon on the Mount as the rule for the future Kingdom but as having no meaning for the Christian today. This view is based on a misinterpretation of the Kingdom. Furthermore, honest Bible study reveals that all the principles taught in this sermon are also taught in the Pauline epistles which these Christians apply today. The only consistent position is to accept the teachings of Christ in this sermon as his will for his disciples.

Let us now project the first beatitude into the Sermon on the Mount as the first theme upon which Jesus makes further comment. In Matthew 5:13-20 we discover how one who is poor in spirit behaves himself. This behavior is shown in three ways.

When we are poor in spirit we live in unselfish service.

> You are like the salt for the earth. If the salt loses its taste, there is no way to make it salty again. It has become worthless; so it is thrown away and people walk on it. You are like light for the world. A city built on a high hill cannot be hid. Nobody lights a lamp to put it under a bowl; instead he puts it on the lamp-stand, where it gives light for everyone in the house. In the same way your light must shine before people, so that they will see the good things you do and give praise to your Father in heaven. (Matthew 5:13-16)

Jesus uses word pictures to express the meaning of humility. First he describes us as salt. There is one significant thing about salt—it has value in what it does to something else. It may add taste, preserve, or cleanse, but its value is in not being alone. So the Christian is one who finds his value in enriching lives. The Christian does not live in isolation. Living in the world, he is not of the world. His relation is one of wholesome influence in society. In fact, the Christian is to be a conscience in society, a service to those around him. Humility is not an attitude of worthlessness but a recognition of true worth. Salt is different from the medium in which it is placed. This difference is our very strength. The text reads, "You are like the salt for the earth." Peter says of us, "But you are the chosen race, the King's priests, the holy nation, God's own people, chosen to proclaim the wonderful acts of God, who called you from the darkness into his own marvelous light" (I Peter 2:9). In commenting on this Martyn Lloyd-Jones says:

> I suggest to you, therefore, that the Christian is to function as the salt of the earth in a much more individual sense, . . . by just being the man that he is in every sphere in which he find himself. For instance, a number of people may be talking together in a rather unworthy manner. Suddenly a Christian enters into the company, and people begin to modify their language. He is already acting as salt, . . . controlling the tendency to putrefaction and pollution. Just by being a Christian, . . . he is already controlling that evil that was manifesting itself, and he does so in every sphere and in every situation. . . .
>
> The primary task of the Church is to evangelize and to

preach the gospel. . . . If the church is always denouncing one particular section of society, she is shutting the evangelistic door upon that section. If we take the New Testament view . . . we must believe that the communist has a soul to be saved in exactly the same way as everybody else. It is my business as a preacher of the gospel, and a representative of the Church, to evangelize all kinds and conditions and classes of men and women. The moment the Church begins to intervene in these political, social and economic matters, therefore, she is hampering and hindering herself in her God-appointed task of evangelism. She can no longer say that she "knows no man after the flesh," and thereby she is sinning. Let the individual play his part as a citizen, and belong to any political party that he may choose. That is something for the individual to decide. The Church is not concerned as a Church about these things. Our business is to preach the gospel and to bring this message of salvation to all.[1]

Secondly, he describes the believer as a light to the world. Like salt, light has a single purpose, not to be seen but to help others to see. Its value is in its effect upon darkness, its contribution to others to help them. One who is poor in spirit lives in unselfish service. His life, like light, penetrates the hopelessness of life for many about him. Lest you feel discouraged that this penetration is so limited, it may be asked, "How much darkness does it take to put out a light?" Remember Jesus made this remarkable statement to very average people, "You are like light for the world." It is a thrill to realize the importance of just being Christian in the world.

As disciples we are a light to the world. This is a

[1] *Studies in the Sermon on the Mount,* Vol. I, pp. 155, 156.

positive, active function of guidance to the way of Christ. We must avoid a pietism which majors in personal peace and minors in public morality. We do not ask what social need has to do with Christian faith, but what Christian faith can do to correct social need. Discipleship is more than being a conscience in society; it adds direction. A conscience often speaks only negatively, passing judgment on actions on the basis of learned values. While this is important, it is even more important to have a prophetic influence, offering society interpretation and direction for the future. Sharing in the service of Christ means that we know which way the world should be going.

Light removes the dimness and uncertainty of life. In the world men trust knowledge to supply light for life. From the Renaissance of the fifteenth century and the Enlightenment of the eighteenth to the present, men have trusted knowledge to serve as the light of life. But Jesus said the light is in simple believers. The world itself is in darkness, and never more so than today. Christ as the light of the world is calling his disciples to recognize their role to reflect his light to the world in which they live. I must take with all seriousness his words, "You are like light for the world."

Two things are essential to the lamp: the oil and the wick. We can be lights only as the oil of the Spirit is present in our lives, and as the lamp wick is trimmed and burning. One of the greater needs of the Church is genuine holiness, a life through which the Spirit of Christ can express the meaning of Christ. But in an emphasis on holiness it is important to see the meaning of the Sermon on the Mount as the way to a whole life. This quality of newness of life will cause men to glorify our Father in heaven.

When we are poor in spirit we confess a divine will above our own.

> Do not think that I have come to do away with the Law of Moses and the teaching of the prophets. I have not come to do away with them, but to give them real meaning. Remember this! As long as heaven and earth last, the least point or the smallest detail of the Law will not be done away with—not until the end of all things. (Matthew 5:17-18)

The proud mind finds it difficult to acknowledge the authority of Christ in his life. But if we would live for Christ, we must commit ourselves to the lordship, or authority, of Christ. A disciple has settled this question affirmatively for his own life. This isn't easy—but it must be my stance as a disciple. As a consequence, my approach to the Scriptures as a disciple is unique. I must come to the Scriptures with my mind already made up to obey it. The challenge is now to hear it correctly, to know what the Lord is actually saying.

As we emphasize the unfolding of God's revelation and the fulfillment of his self-disclosure in the New Testament, we recognize levels between the Testaments. Throughout the Old Testament, God had something more and more to say about himself. In the New Testament, Christ as God is the full word!

As the full revelation of God and his will, Jesus gives us the final interpretation of God's will. The Incarnation has brought God into our life experience. He himself lived the will of God. Here Jesus says, "I have not come to do away with them [the Law or the teaching of the prophets], but to give them real meaning" (Matthew 5: 17). He came to fill the Scriptures full, to give us their full meaning. By his words, "You have heard. . . . But now I tell you," he was not removing what God had said in history but was giving us the more complete meaning. The Old Testament is related to the New Testament as promise to fulfillment. Christ is the culmination of God's self-disclosure, and he is the full expression of God's willl. One who is poor in spirit, who confesses Jesus as Lord, will live by Jesus' outline of the will of God.

The Christian Church must rediscover the authority and power of God's Word. We have no other way to understand God correctly other than through his own revelation. Our only certainty that what we are experiencing in religious exercises is actually God is when we test the experience by God's Word. We are only as spiritual as we are scriptural. But since we tend to impose our culture upon the Word, let us beware of domesticating God's Word to conform to our wishes. We must always test what we think to be his Word by relating our concepts to the personification of that Word in Jesus Christ.

When we are poor in spirit we confess our need of a righteousness above our own.

> Therefore, who ever disobeys even the smallest of the commandments, and teachers others to do the same, will be least in the Kingdom of heaven. On the other hand, whoever obeys the Law, and teaches others to do the same, will be great in the Kingdom of heaven. I tell you, then, that you will be able to enter the Kingdom of heaven only if you are more faithful than the teachers of the Law and the Pharisees in doing what God requires. (Matthew 5:19-20)

There is a righteousness of the law that one can seek to achieve—the Pharisees are representative of those who did so and made religion an end in itself. Yet they missed the basic spirit of the law which said that all of life is to begin with God (Exodus 20:1-2). Jesus said to them, "You study the Scriptures because you think that in them you will find eternal life. . . . Yet you refuse to come to me that you may have life" (John 5:39-40). Our Lord made not only positive statements but also negative ones. He exposed false teaching as clearly as he outlined the truth. He is the one in whom we understand righteousness. Throughout the sermon this is a recurring theme.

God's righteousness is found only in Christ; the experience of righteousness is by entering into right relation with him. Here Jesus says, "You will be able to enter the Kingdom of heaven only if you are more faithful than [exceeding the righteousness of, the King James Version says] the teachers of the Law and the Pharisees in doing what God requires" (Matthew 5:20). We cannot exceed them in quantity of deeds as expressions of obedience to holy laws. What then is his point? We can exceed them in quality of faith, in an identification with God by faith that relates to his person and not only to his precepts.

In the writings of one who had been a Pharisee, who had lived "so far as a man can be righteous by obeying the commands of the Law, . . . without fault" (Philippians 3:6), there is a clear distinction between this establishing of one's own righteousness and sharing the righteousness of Christ. Paul's formula for the latter is threefold: "For we worship God by his Spirit, and rejoice in our life in Christ Jesus. We do not put any trust in external ceremonies" (Philippians 3:3). One who is poor in spirit finds his fulfillment in Christ, not in himself.

Christ was not simply offering us another law, he was offering us himself. Righteousness, or right relatedness with God, is now an actual experience, not something we keep working toward. This is the basis for the Beatitudes, the reason Christ could pronounce blessing on common folk who were humble enough to open their lives to God. This is what Paul calls "the righteousness that comes from God, and is based on faith" (Philippians 3:9).

Righteous living is the expression of a right relationship. Knowing the fruit of the Spirit is itself the fulfillment of the higher law of God. When we live by this love, we are keeping his commandments. To love God is to put him first, to worship him as the highest reality, to serve him rather than use him; it is to give him a rightful share of your time. These are the first four of the

Ten Commandments. To live by love to one's fellows fulfills the meaning of the other six commandments: to honor one's parents, to safeguard life rather than to take it, to respect persons and not use them, to respect the rights and possessions of others, to regard the reputation of another with integrity, and to rejoice in others' blessings rather than wish to take from them. The disciple of Christ is free from the constraint of the law for righteousness because he lives in the love of Christ.

Jesus said, "You can do nothing without me." Only as the branch abides in the vine does it bear fruit. (John 15:1-10.) It is through our being "in Christ" that we have our fruit unto righteousness. "Set free from sin . . . [we] are the slaves of God" (Romans 6:22). This is an attitude of faith, not simply of intellectual faith, but of total trust. We have learned by being honest about our sins that we cannot "save ourselves by ourselves"; Christ saves us. And his saving us is a present reality; I have found that I need the presence and power of God constantly if I am to express the life of God through my life.

This assurance of salvation does not mean that we have no questions as disciples. If we would have a vital faith, we must be honest in admitting our doubts. What is faith if it is not response to evidence without absolute proof? I have found that to admit doubt and face it honestly does not mean that I must now doubt everything —believe my doubts! Descartes held that if you would be a real seeker after truth, you must at one time in your life doubt all things. But Sören Kierkegaard said this is "as foolish as thinking you must make a man lie in a heap in order to teach him to stand up straight. We are only beating the air when we say we are struggling with doubt when it is insubordination, refusal to obey, to accept authority."

The arrogant cut themselves off from close friends; the humble can share fully with others. Similarly, this is true in relating to God. It is our pride which gets in the way of open fellowship. God says, "I dwell in the high and holy place, with him also that is of a contrite and humble spirit" (Isaiah 57:15). Blessed, spiritually prosperous—*happy*—are the poor in spirit, is the promise of the Master.

I open my hand, Lord
  to take from thee;
Your Word becomes my will,
  your life, my example;
In faith I'll follow thee.

3

Happy Are Those Who Mourn

Happy are those who mourn [take sin seriously]: God will comfort them! (Matthew 5:4)

To mourn is to feel deeply, to care about evil, to deplore some existing wrong. Jesus pronounces his blessing upon those who take sin seriously. In fact you and I grow spiritually only by being honest about the problems of sin in our lives and dealing with them. As Viktor Frankl quoted a Jewish saying, "Man can recognize the forgiveness of Heaven for a sin only by his never committing this sin again." [1]

As an X ray reveals disorder in the body, so the words of Christ in the next section of his sermon expose the perversions in our lives. Jesus himself took evil seriously;

[1] Viktor E. Frankl, *The Doctor and the Soul* (New York: Knopf, 1965), p. 59.

he didn't gloss it over. To care deeply about social injustice as well as personal sins is always right. The beatitude of mourning calls for an attitude of repentance, of genuine concern over our problems. This is a mourning of inadequacy, of human limitations, of travail of the soul. Such an attitude means that I change my mind about my behavior toward God and toward man.

Personal healing comes through mourning, for in this exercise hidden resentments surface and are resolved. Old bitterness always has new consequences because it is never really forgotten. Often in counseling, the counselor can help the person seeking advice to rebuild crippled areas only after the mourning of confession. The correction of one's life does not come without deep readjustments of soul and conscience. Many of us are "uptight" about happenings from which we could have release if we would be honest with God. His comfort is not a sham; he will help us resolve our problems. God forgives, but only as we repent lest his mercy be a pseudo-forgiveness which leaves us in our perversions.

We should not think of sin only in legal or moralistic terms. The depth of sin is what it does to persons. First of all, sin alters one's own life. It keeps us from being our best. Sin is a perversion of the good. Sin is always taking the lesser way.

Jesus didn't come just to save us from problems we have but from the problem we are! We are the problem—in selfishness, prejudice, status-seeking, power struggles, hostility, and violence. We like to have our own way. The prophet Isaiah says, "All we like sheep have gone astray; we have turned every one to his own way" (Isaiah 53:6). This is our problem—putting our way ahead of God's way.

We will now observe in this passage how seriously a Kingdom member takes sin. Jesus applies this in several areas.

First we see how seriously a Kingdom member takes the sin of emotional violence.

> You have heard that men were told in the past, "Do not murder; anyone who commits murder will be brought before the judge." But now I tell you: whoever is angry with his brother will be brought before the judge; whoever calls his brother "You good-for-nothing!" will be brought before the Council; and whoever calls his brother a worthless fool will be in danger of going to the fire of hell.
>
> So if you are about to offer your gift to God at the altar and there you remember that your brother has something against you, leave your gift there in front of the altar and go at once to make peace with your brother; then come back and offer your gift to God.
>
> If a man brings a lawsuit against you and takes you to court, be friendly with him while there is time, before you get to court; once you are there he will turn you over to the judge, who will hand you over to the police, and you will be put in jail. There you will stay, I tell you, until you pay the last penny of your fine. (Matthew 5:21-26)

Jesus takes the injunction, "Thou shalt not kill," and fills it full of meaning, saying in essence, "Anything that leads to killing is wrong—anger, envy, jealousy, bitterness." Christ calls us to avoid not only violence of act but also violence of spirit. Our attitude toward others is to be one of love, of sincere concern for their welfare.

It is not only possible to feel deeply about evil, but it is necessary that we do so. It is right to be angry about social injustice But it is important that when we get angry about issues we don't take that anger out on people. Jesus in the Temple was angry about an issue and concerned for the people. He used the whip on the animals, not on the people (see Luke 2:15). In Paul's letter to the Ephesians he writes, "If you become angry, do not let your anger lead you into sin" (Ephesians 4:26). With the awareness that an emotionally upset person needs release lest he harbor this and become bitter, Paul adds, "Do not stay angry all day." An angry person makes a very poor counselor.

The answer to emotional violence is genuine love. The priority is given to others when you live by love. In fact, Jesus becomes very explicit on this. "If you are about to offer your gift to God at the altar and there you remember your brother has something against you, leave your gift to God at the altar and go at once to make peace with your brother; then come back and offer your gift to God" (Matthew 5:23-24). You can't offer a gift to God when there is a wrong spirit in your life. Our sense of worship is often dulled by the clouded emotions of our own lives. Only as we purge ourselves of hurt feelings, of bitterness, anger, or envy, can we enter into the joy of a free spirit.

Jesus asks that we love not only our friends, but our enemies as well. Love for one's enemies is a positive and costly approach to life's greater problems. Such love must be creative; it must find the way to build bridges of understanding and involvement. God demonstrated this in Christ, ultimately at Calvary, where he opened himself to us.

When Jesus said the first commandment is to love God, to open your life to God, he also said the second commandment is just like it in that you also open your life to your neighbor, be he friend or enemy. While nations of the world, at their sub-Christian levels of behavior, may engage in war, Christians are members of Christ's Kingdom which he is gathering from all nations and belong together as brothers. Brother cannot take the life of brother and claim to be serving the same Lord. "It must be admitted," as Owen Weatherly says, "that under no acceptable standard of morality does one's duty to his own country relieve him of his duty to be equally concerned about the well-being of human life." [2]

As Christians develop a conscience against participation in war and recognize the higher level of life to which we are called, our witness to those who live beneath the will of Christ and participate in war should ultimately make a difference. Too many professed Christians have a conscience on lesser matters with no sense of the evil of war itself. But there are signs of an awakening. Weatherly, who is not committed to nonviolence as I am, says, "For some time our attitude toward war has been growing steadily more realistic. When Machiavelli published

[2] Owen M. Weatherly, *The Ten Commandments in Modern Perspective* (Richmond: John Knox Press, 1961), p. 96.

his eulogies in praise of the virtue of war in the early years of the fifteenth century they were generally accepted as fact. Before the end of the nineteenth century William T. Sherman could say that 'war . . . is . . . hell,' with absolutely no fear of serious contradiction. The sentiment which prevails most widely at the present time was expressed by Major General Smedley D. Butler when he said, 'To Hell with war.' "[3]

Secondly we see how seriously a Kingdom member takes the sin of sexual immorality.

> You have heard that it was said, "Do not commit adultery." But now I tell you: anyone who looks at a woman and wants to possess her is guilty of committing adultery with her in his heart. So if your right eye causes you to sin, take it out and throw it away! It is much better for you to lose a part of your body than to have your whole body thrown into hell. If your right hand causes you to sin, cut it off and throw it away! It is much better for you to lose one of your limbs than to have your whole body go off to hell.
>
> It was also said, "Anyone who divorces his wife must give her a written notice of divorce." But now I tell you: if a man divorces his wife, and she has not been unfaithful, then he is guilty of making her commit adultery if she marries again; and the man who marries her also commits adultery. (Matthew 5:27-32)

Sex is a gift of God for the joy and association of man and woman. Its full delight is found only in genuine love, where two persons give themselves to each other fully

[3] *Ibid.,* p. 98.

in a spiritual commitment of honesty and respect. Sex is perverted when individuals use each other merely as bodies for selfish gratification. There is nothing sinful or shameful about sex or the use of sex, only in its abuse or misuse.

Actually, sexual union is God's gift to complete the emotional and spiritual union of a man and woman in marriage. As Keith Miller says, "The sexual joining of a man and wife is an outward expression of an inner reality—the joining of two lives." [4] Marriage becomes the place of belonging, of absolute trust, the place of security in each other. The one-partner plan for marriage outlined in the New Testament provides both psychological security and the satisfaction of spiritual integrity. If either partner comes to feel that he or she is being used or is being cheated, the security of love is destroyed. Sex is intended by God to be the intimate seal of our complete belonging to each other. As such it is to be enjoyed in freedom between a man and wife.

Sexuality is a beautiful part of the creation of man. A man or woman contributes to life his or her particular strength. Each complements the other. He brings masculine strength to life, with his creativity and aggressive action. She brings an aesthetic dimension with finessee and taste, with her creativity, her spirit of life, and her understanding of the whole. Physical participation in sex is not necessary for sexuality to be appreciated. But in God's order sex itself is good, not sinful.

[4] Keith Miller, *The Second Touch* (Waco, Tex.: Word Books, 1967), p. 95.

Marriage is God's order for the sharing of sex without violating the sanctity of personality. By the nature of our being human personalities, male and female are essentially equal. In his book on the Ten Commandments, Owen M. Weatherly says, "There is nothing in the nature of the human person which gives anyone the right to use another personality—masculine or feminine—as a means to an end." [5] His statement on the meaning of marriage is an appropriate elucidation of this passage. "Marriage is the union of one man with one woman for the purpose of sex fulfillment, the procreation and nurture of children, and the completion of the basic development and expression of personality through ultimate communication and interaction with another human being enough like himself (herself) to be congenial and sufficiently different to be enduringly attractive and stimulating to the point of exciting him (her) toward the fullest and richest possible realization and employment of his (her) potentialities as a person." [6]

Again Jesus gives an old commandment its full meaning. "You have heard that it was said, 'Do not commit adultery.' But now I tell you . . ." anything that leads to adultery is wrong (Matthew 5:27). The word "adultery" has within it the basic idea of infidelity to a vow. In a day when a woman was looked upon as a second-class citizen, Jesus elevated her to equality with man. Now as heirs together of the grace of God they can experience God's goal for marriage—a partnershsip, she in a one-man

[5] *The Ten Commandments in Modern Perspective,* pp. 105-6.
[6] *Ibid.,* p. 104.

and he in a one-woman relation for life. For a man to put away his wife is to break the covenant, to be guilty of adultery. To marry one who is put away is also to participate in the breaking of the marriage covenant—unless, Jesus says, the covenant has already been broken by immorality; then the implication is different.

But Jesus does not speak only in terms of physical immorality. Purity of life is not just a matter of the body but of the mind and heart. For a man in a covenant of marriage to lust after another woman is to be untrue to the covenant with his wife whether there be some other physical relation of sex or not. Jesus is saying anything that leads to adultery is sin. One who lives with lustful thoughts, who feeds his or her mind on contemplations of sensuality with persons outside of his love-covenant, will not be able to bring his best and true self to his companion. This is a psychological fact in marriage relations. It is also true that marriage succeeds because it is a spiritual union, not only a physical one. Don't overlook the fact that one who lives with sex as an obsession never enjoys it anyway.

Proper sexual behavior depends on proper thinking. "As a man thinketh . . . so is he." (Proverbs 23:7.) Purity of behavior is dependent upon purity of thought. The modern obsession with sex has supplied the public with a diet, both by literature and by screen, which warps the adherent's life. One does not achieve the greater happiness of love if his thinking is constantly filled with lustful imaginations. Love means that my life is intimately open to my companion, but it also means that I will bring my very best self to her. Sexual experience is then a partnership of love, a delighting in one another, not a lustful exploiting of one another.

Too often we interpret this passage so moralistically that we condemn only the extra-marital sex relation. If some married person has an affair with a third party, the illegal sex involvement is serious. But even more serious is what the person is doing against his or her companion and family. Divorce and remarriage have their most serious sin in breaking a covenant relation with its responsibilities.

In spite of the trial-and-error patterns of modern society the values of marriage for life are still the highest. What persons can become in a wholesome marriage is of greater importance. In view of this it is imperative that the Christian hold the highest ideals and practices of courtship. Love is for life, and one's love makes him what he is and what he becomes!

Thirdly we see how seriously a Kingdom member takes the sin of mental dishonesty.

You have also heard that men were told in the past, "Do not break your promise, but do what you have sworn to do before the Lord." But now I tell you: do not use any vow when you make a promise; do not swear by heaven, because is it God's throne; nor by earth, because it is the resting place for his feet; nor by Jerusalem, because it is the city of the great King. Do not even swear by your head, because you cannot make a single hair white or black. Just say "Yes" or "No"—anything else you have to say comes from the Evil One. (Matthew 5:33-37)

Again Jesus says, "You have also heard. . . . But now I tell you . . . do not use any vow." One's mental perspective determines the way he operates in relation to authority. Swearing is basically an attempt to support the authority of one's words by appeal to another authority. But Jesus maximizes the value of the person and the integrity of the individual. His admonition, "Do not use any vow," is matched by his command, "Just say 'Yes' or 'No.' " The command of Christ is for us to be strictly honest in word of life. The believer's word is as good as any oath he can swear, and for this reason, many of us as Christians do not take any oath but simply affirm, a privilege provided by the laws of our land for all legal transactions. But more than that, affirming is testimony of one's commitment to absolute honesty. I choose to affirm rather than to swear.

More significantly Jesus is saying three things about the evil of swearing. First, swearing is *irreverent*, for it is using God to support our purposes. We do not use God, that is, try to make him to serve us; we serve him. Second, swearing is *irrelevant,* for it doesn't change anything. One does not alter the course of life by swearing, nor does one cause God to adjust his will. Third, swearing is *unnecessary* when a person is honest. The honest man doesn't need the oath and the dishonest one doesn't honor it.

The Scriptures say that God honors his Word above his name. Likewise we are to understand the importance of our words. There is a direct relation between the way a man expresses himself and how he thinks of himself. So Jesus adds, anything needed beyond your normal honest communication is there on account of evil. We don't let evil determine our life-style!

As Kingdom members we are to take sin seriously. Repentance is an attitude of life that not only acknowledges sin but renounces it. The apostle Paul, in Romans 6:3, makes clear that one who is "baptized into union with Christ Jesus" participates in the meaning of both the death and the resurrection of Christ. Identifying with him in death, we die to the old life in which we once lived. That is, we break with the old life in which sin reigned—a break as definite as death! But beyond this we share his resurrection. That is, we participate in a new life which shares the victory of Christ. In this relationship God releases us from the "old man" and makes of us new men.

Not to take sin seriously is to identify with the old life. But there is a way of deliverance from practicing sin. John writes. "Whoever is a child of God does not continue to sin, because God's very nature is in him; and because God is his Father, he is not able to continue to sin" (I John 3:9).

Taking sin seriously means that we recognize the problem for what it is and recognize our need for God's power to overcome it. It is imperative that we be honest about our inability to correct the problem by ourselves. The story is told of a man seen grocery shopping in the supermarket, pushing a cart down the aisle between the stacks of groceries with a little boy in the basket of the cart crying insistently. A lady heard the man talking as he went along, "Keep calm, Albert, don't make a scene, Albert." Some minutes later she was at the check-out counter when he came up, cart piled high with groceries, child still crying, and the man speaking emphatically in low tones, "Keep calm, Albert; don't make a scene, control yourself, Albert." The lady said, "Sir, I'm amazed at how calmly you keep speaking to that child when he doesn't pay any attention to you." The man replied, "Lady, you don't understand—I'm Albert."

Rather than talk our way through a problem we can appropriate God's grace to overcome it. If we take sin as seriously as God asks us to, we'll bring it to him for deliverance. He alone can deliver us and give us the comfort of freedom. John writes, "But if we live in the light—just as he is in the light—then we have fellowship one with another [the believer and God], and the blood of Jesus Christ, his Son, makes us clean [keeps on cleansing us] from every sin" (I John 1:7). By identifying with Christ we stand on the victory side of the Cross. The promise is that Christ's deliverance through the Cross will keep on functioning in our lives to separate us from sin. "Thanks be to God! . . . We are always led by God as prisoners in Christ's victory procession" (II Corinthians 2:14).

4

Happy Are the Meek

Happy are the meek: they will receive what God has promised! (Matthew 5:5)

These are strange words for an age in which men think first of power and status. Caught up in the struggle for supremacy we minimize the development of character, of personality and integrity. Jesus is talking of a style of life that is radically different from life in society, from life outside of his fellowship. This is a style of life that is spiritual, that maximizes the true worth of a man. This life-style sees the spirit-values of life as primary values, such as love, friendship, joy, peace, forgiveness, and purpose.

Meekness is not weakness; it is rather the greatness of spirit that looks beyond one's self, beyond the immediate. Meekness is patience, gentleness, forbearance, yielding to a greater good. Meekness acknowledges that truth is bigger than one's self, that others are important, that persons are worth more than things. Meekness stands in uncompromising fidelity to truth without being defensive, for it reecognizes the greatness of truth itself. Meekness operates on the premise that there are beliefs big enough to die for. A meek person would rather die than sin, would rather die than ruin another for whom Christ died.

No standard which Christ gives us is more difficult for the natural man than this. We seem to have been born with our fists clenched. We interpret life as though it is cowardice not to defend one's self. We forget that taking life to preserve material things is to elevate material values above the value of persons. Here our materialism catches up with us. Life is given every day in the Labor market for monetary returns, and it is easy for man to then place a monetary value on another's life. One cannot understand this passage fully unless he comes to it with the perspective of Christ—that persons are the most valuable things in the world. Emmanuel Kant, marking the great watershed of philosophy which moved us into the modern period, expresses this as a categorical imperative: "Treat very person as an end in himself and not as a means to an end."

Meekness thinks in terms of the need of others rather than the defense of self.

You have heard that it was said, "An eye for an eye, and a tooth for a tooth." But now I tell you: do not take revenge on someone who does you wrong. If anyone slaps you on the right cheek, let him slap your left cheek too. (Matthew 5:38-39)

As disciples of Christ we will elevate others above ourselves. Instead of being occupied in resisting evil we will engage in releasing good. We should not wait for problems, tensions, and war to develop and then defend ourselves. Rather we should work in a preventive way by spreading love and goodwill. Rather than being on the defensive we can take the offensive. Love is a strategy of operation that takes the initiative, that seeks to win the neighbor to Christ.

To resist evil with violence is to let evil set the pace or outline the front, the level of operation. As a consequence of such an approach the life of the disciple would be pulled down to the level of evil. But the disciple has his own mandate. His level of operation is the righteousness of Christ. Nonviolent resistance to evil frees one to meet and overcome evil on another ground. Nonviolence to evil is essentiial if one is to avoid becoming entrapped at a lower level of operation. Only by the stance of nonviolent resistance is one free to operate on the higher level of love and justice. True justice seeks the correction of problems, at the social level as well as the personal. Furthermore, it does so by the transformation of lives, as Jesus does through Calvary.

Love is not passive; it is active. Turning the other cheek is not surrender; it is a strategy of operation. Hatred is always at a disadvantage when met by love. In fact hatred is often disarmed by love. The place where love is limited is at the impersonal level, for there the strength of love cannot be shown. Hatred can be impersonal; it can be fed by negatives, by denunciations. A revolutionary finds it nearly impossible to love persons.

Too often we love people in the abstract and hate persons! True love is personal and grows by personal contact and involvement. God did not call to us from heaven to declare that he loves us; God came in Christ to involve himself in our situation and express his love for us, to lay down his life in his love for us.

Meekness thinks in terms of personalities rather than material gain.

> And if someone takes you to court to sue you for your shirt, let him have your coat as well. And if one of the occupation troops forces you to carry his pack one mile, carry it another mile. When someone asks you for something, give it to him; when someone wants to borrow something, lend it to him. (Matthew 5:40-42)

The disciple elevates persons above the material. Christian faith maximizes the value of the individual. Both communism and capitalism regard the individual as quite worthless in the achievement of their different goals. But the disciple of Christ sees the individual as having ultimate worth. Man, as a spiritual being, as a living soul, is more valuable than all else in the world. This means that cultivating personality and friends is far more important than collecting things.

Status in life is better measured by the character of one's friends than by the amount of one's material possessions. When one dies the question is not, "How much did he leave?"—for he left all of it. The question is, "How many mourn his passing?" Billy Sunday said a man ought to "live so that even the undertaker will miss him when he's gone."

Love means involvement, participation with others. God in love involved himself in man's predicament, even though it cost him the Cross. Love looks beyond the problem to the person. God cares about us so much he isn't "hung up" over what we've done. He is able to separate the issue from the person. Love enables us to always work for the good of persons and their discovery of wholeness in God's grace.

Jesus' words make the application of this truth quite practical. If a man takes your shirt give him your coat too—let him know that a good relationship with him is worth more to you than the material things. If a man compels you to go one mile with him, go two. In this act, love is a strategy of operation. In going the second mile one now has the advantage in communicating meaning. The other person will now be asking, "What makes this man different?"

If one asks help, give it. It does not always follow that what he asks is what you give. A disciple is neither stupid nor a stooge. One who is in Christ operates by spiritual discernment and wisdom, and helps a man not by giving him what he wants but what he may need. Above all, our response is one of caring and sharing; we are ready to serve, to get involved. This is the risk and the cost of love.

Meekness thinks of behavior as a service rather than a bargain.

You have heard that it was said, "Love your friends, hate your enemies." But now I tell you: love your enemies, and pray for those who mistreat you, so that you will become the sons of your Father in heaven. For he makes his sun to shine on bad and good people alike, and gives rain to those who do right and those who do wrong. Why should you expect God to reward you, if you love only the people who love you? Even the tax collectors do that! And if you speak only to your friends, have you done anything out of the ordinary? Even the pagans do that! You must be perfect—just as your Father in heaven is perfect. (Matthew 5:43-48)

Love doesn't hate enemies: it asks why there are enemies. In meekness it seeks to win them as friends. This is the plus of Christian experience. To love those who love us is no different from the behavior of sinners all about us. But to love our enemies, to reach out to those unlike ourselves, is to share the Calvary love by which God overcame our hostility to make us his friends.

John Horsch tells of an old Mennonite minister in the Emmenthal, Canton Berne. In the days when this Free Church group was being severely persecuted, this man acted in love toward his enemies. Early one morning he heard men on the house roof, tearing off the tiles and throwing them to the ground to force him to move out. Arising from bed he asked his wife to prepare a good breakfast for the men. Then he went outside and invited them to breakfast, insisting that they come in and eat since they had been working. Shamefacedly they came in and sat at the table. He prayed for them and their families, then served them breakfast. When they had eaten they went out and put the tiles back on the roof.

In the words of an old Swedish hymn.

> There is nothing that is not won,
> By the love which suffers.

Our philosophy of life as disciples is to serve our fellows, to enrich all of life. By contrast, a selfish life eventually shrinks to mere existence. In loving others, accepting their abuse so that we can exhibt Christ's spirit, we are able to win them to God. In fact the disciple expects persecution. The Bible says, "All who want to live a godly life in union with Christ Jesus will be persecuted" (II Timothy 3:12). Righteous living reminds people of the claims of God upon their lives, often calling forth some of the same hostility that was expressed against Jesus.

The Master closes this section by saying, "You must be perfect—just as your Father in heaven is perfect." This is a perfection of love, to treat all men with grace, friends or enemies. This is the course of action for those who represent the Lord.

It will help us better understand the role of the meek in society if we can understand the relation of Church and State. The Church operates under the mandate of Christ at the highest possible level in his will, while the State operates by God's order but on a secular level beneath the full will of Christ. The line is not drawn vertically, with the Church on the right and the State on the left, both equally doing the service of God. The line should be drawn horizontally, showing the Church to be at a higher level, answering to the mandate of Christ, while the State is on a lower level answering to the people. True, the "powers" are ordained of God (Romans 13:1-10); they are in God's order but they are ordained of God; he is still above the powers. There are times in which we ought to obey God rather than men. The meek person is one whose priorities are established by his being a member of the Kingdom of Christ. He is a servant in this world, not a status-seeker.

Those who truly live by Christ's will inherit the earth, and will come to enjoy what God really intended for life. This is the paradox: "Whoever tries to gain his own life will lose it; whoever loses his life for my sake will gain it" (Matthew 10:39).

5

Happy Are Those Who Do What God Requires

Happy are those whose greatest desire is to do what God requires: God will satisfy them fully! (Matthew 5:6)

Having been created in the image of God, in and for fellowship with God, our lives are incomplete apart from him. Just as no person can fully be a person without other people, so none of us is complete in fulfilling his potential without God. Some think that walking with God narrows the life, but the truth of the matter is that God frees us for larger living. It is selfishness and sin that close us in, that isolate the individual.

Dr. Adler, a rather conceited professor, was at a dinner party one evening and in the after-dinner conversation the discussion went against him. He got up in a huff and left the room, slamming the door behind him. In the silence that followed, someone, wishing to relieve the embarrassment of the hostess, said, "Well, he's gone." She replied, "No, he isn't; that's a closet." Slamming out of God's presence only closes one into a narrower existence.

To hunger for righteousness is to want a right relation with God himself. Jesus came to bring God to us and to bring us to God. In fact Jesus is our righteousness, for he is the one in whom we come into right relation with God. This is an authentic rightness, for we are identifying with him. We are not simply trying to keep religious laws well enough that we will gain his acceptance. But in this right relation we live in a manner that expresses the life of Christ.

The test of one's faith is whether he makes religion an end in itself or whether he moves beyond the religious form or symbol to God himself. We need symbols to help us in communication, understanding, and fellowship. Symbols can be religious rites, religious patterns, or religious words. But we must distinguish between the symbol and the meaning. We must be certain that we are worshiping God.

It is easy to outline the extent of our fellowship by having common symbols, but this can result in our idolizing the symbol and failing to experience true community in Christ. We must see symbol as only symbol, and then transcend it by maximizing the truth of being in Christ. Wherever symbol becomes an end in itself, Christianity is domesticated and loses its dynamic. Christian faith refuses to stop short of God himself.

Hunger for God transforms service from exhibition to devotion.

Be careful not to perform your religious duties in public so that people will see what you do. If you do these things publicly you will not have any reward from your Father in Heaven.

So when you give something to a needy person, do not make a big show of it, as the show-offs do in the synagogues and on the streets. They do it so that people will praise them. Remember this! They have already been paid in full. But when you help a needy person, do it in such a way that even your closest friend will not know about it, but it will be a private matter. And your Father, who sees what you do in private, will reward you. (Matthew 6:1-4)

Notice Jesus' frequent reference to God as "Father." True religion is not a form but a fellowship. Hungering for God means that we are concerned to know him, not merely things about him. And this is the quality of knowledge Jesus came to bring. He was able to say to the disciples, "Whoever has seen me has seen the Father."

Jesus is speaking in this passage about religious service, giving alms, ministering to those in need. Again his emphasis is on motive. Our purpose in service is not to be admired by men but to extend the work of our Father. We can recall the occasion when Jesus and the disciples sat watching men cast their gifts into the temple treasury in a manner so open that the size of their contributions was obvious. In contrast the poor widow surreptitiously dropped in two mites, actually all that she had. Jesus complimented her gift because of the spirit of devotion that prompted it. Now contrast her actions with the larger contributions made without this motive. Talented persons who serve in prominent positions are not necessarily rendering their contribution in the greater spirit.

Prayer is a vigorous force of service. But prayer is not ordering God or asking God to do things our way or by our time schedule. Prayer for others and with others is a service—a part of which benefits one's own life, enabling him to be a better person in relation to others. Under a rather trying experience I once found myself praying, "Dear Lord, I need patience, and I need it right now!"

The best things of life cannot be hurried. Devotion is expressed in our trust that God is working his will in us. Phillips Brooks, a New England preacher, failed as a schoolteacher, but this became his turning point to success. As one of the greatest North American preachers he learned patience in God's school. He was known for his poise, yet those who worked with him knew of times when he was frustrated and irritable. Finding him pacing the floor one day a visitor asked him what was wrong. "The trouble is," Dr. Brooks answered, "that I'm in a hurry, but God isn't."

Another significant thing is seen in Jesus' reference to reward. Men who serve for the applause of men get their reward when they receive that applause. Men who serve for the glory of God get their reward from God himself, sharing the glory of his grace with them. Christians are self-contradictory when they reject discipleship with its works of faith, lest they place too much emphasis on works or obedience, yet at the same time they over-emphasize working for rewards. The reward of serving God is the joy of his presence and blessing. Just to be in his fellowship is reward.

Hunger for God transforms prayer from performance to communion.

> And when you pray, do not be like the show-offs! They love to stand up and pray in the synagogues and on the street corners so that everybody will see them. Remember this! They have already been paid in full. But when you pray, go to your room and close the door, and pray to your Father, who is unseen. And your Father, who sees what you do in private, will reward you. (Matthew 6:5-6)

Someone has said, "Prayer is not overcoming God's reluctance, it is laying hold on God's willingness." Prayer is not talking God into doing something. Rather, prayer is giving God the moral freedom to move in the life of a person whom he respects as a free moral agent. It is letting God do in your life what he has wanted to do whenever you would respond. Prayer is sharing with God, it is acknowledging one's need of him, it is participating in his work.

The seat of our problem of spiritual apathy is in our lack of prayer. It is said that Martin Luther prayed four hours each day to be enabled to accomplish his labors. Helmut Thielicke, a German evangelical, says, "To work without praying and without listening means only to grow and spread one's self upward, without striking roots and without any equivalent in the earth."[1] Our problem, he says, is not in our nerves but in our roots, stunted and starved.

The prayer of faith takes the initiative in bringing God's presence and power into a situation where men forced him out or withstood him. Paul says, "We are not fighting against human beings, but against the wicked spiritual forces in the heavenly world, the rulers, authorities, and cosmic powers of this dark age" (Ephesians 6:12). When we pray, we invite God to act in a setting where Satan has prevented others from asking him. For example, think of how Elijah took the initiative. He asked God to shut the heavens that there be no rain, called down fire on the altar to evidence that the living God was at work, and prayed for rain lest it be thought that the drought was happenstance. He dared to bring God's power to bear upon a sinful society. When we take the initiative in true faith, we find that God is there walking with us. I have found this to be true in evangelism, moving into situations beyond my abilities, but moving in faith and finding that God is there honoring his promises.

Again, Jesus makes clear that prayer is not a pretense. Prayer is not a show of piety, something done for the attention of men. A disciple is never a "holy man" on exhibition. A disciple is one who, like his Master, sincerely and authentically shares his total life with God. As Elton Trueblood says, "Part of the significance of these words lies not only in the avoidance of the distraction

[1] Helmut Thielicke, *The Waiting Father* (New York: Harper, 1959), p. 65.

that other peoople create, but, even more in the elimination of the temptation to make the spiritual life a matter of display or ostentation. The great value of being alone in our deepest experience is that solitariness transcends the tendency to try to impress." [2]

Prayer is the occasion of meeting God, sharing in secret so that in the open expression it will be evident that one is walking with God. If one does not spend time in private prayer it may indicate that it is not to God but to religion that he is relating. A great testimony to John Baillie's faith is given by his wife, who said three things in his study characterized his life: the desk where he wrote, the chair where he read, and the pad where he knelt to pray.

Dr. Trueblood says, "If spiritual intercourse with another finite individual is an amazing leap across a chasm, which separates the personalities even of those who love each other dearly, intercourse with the Infinite Person is more amazing, because the chasm that separates us is incalculably greater. A man who prays is engaging in the most ambitious of all undertakings, and therefore he needs all of the help he can get." [3] For this reason the teachings of Christ on prayer are of supreme importance. His own personal example becomes our greatest guide—Jesus prayed!

[2] Elton Trueblood, *The New Man for Our Time* (New York: Harper, 1970), pp. 72-73.

[3] *Ibid.*, p. 73.

Hunger for God transforms prayer from impressionism to personalism.

In your prayers do not use a lot of words, as the pagans do, who think that God will hear them because of their long prayers. Do not be like them; your Father already knows what you need before you ask him. (Matthew 6:7-8)

There is little reason to try to impress God by our mannerisms in prayer for he looks at the heart. Vain repetition is an insult to the Father who wants to meet us and share himself with us. It is when we stop talking and listen that we hear him. This is why one can find the way to effective prayer by praying over the Scriptures. As one reads God's Word, he can learn the art of meditation, waiting on the Holy Spirit to impress and stimulate his thinking about God's will and purpose. It is under the Spirit's anointing that "old men shall dream dreams and young men shall see visions" (Joel 2:28).

"Far from prayer being a matter of words, it is often, at its best, freedom from words," says Trueblood, "since our own chatter can prevent our listening." The same author challenges us to learn from saints of God who have demonstrated the way and power of prayer. He says that some begin the day by saying, " 'Lord, I am ready to listen. Speak to me now.' Then the individual waits in a quiet of vibrant attention." [4]

This concept of prayer as conversation, of listening to God, is the key to discovering his will. This is the very

[4] *Ibid.*, p. 73.

opposite of vain repetition. Having witnessed the prayer flags of the Tibetan Buddhists waving in the breeze to offer the many prayers written on them and their prayer wheels filled with hundreds of prayers to be offered at every rotation, or the many repetitions of various other religions, I find it becomes clear what Jesus means by vain repetition. But this happens among us as we run by often repeated phrases and call it prayer. God is waiting to meet us, not simply to hear our words. Jesus says God knows what we need before we ask him—but he wants us in his fellowship.

Blessed are those who hunger for God—they can meet him. He isn't hard to find. That is to say, if any man really wants to meet God, he can. But remember, God doesn't simply want your service; he wants you. Conversely, true faith doesn't just want things from God; it wants to be with God. Love causes one to want to share in the life of, or to be in the presence of, the one who is loved. Prayer is at its best a deep-level fellowship. This is why it has been said, "The school of prayer is one from which no person ever graduates."

In honest commitment, I yield as much of myself as I understand today, to as much of God as I understand today. This is honest realism and intelligent relation to the psychology of Christian growth and to the degree of knowledge of God that I have at a given time. And this is all that God expects. Normal Christian growth is a harmonious relationship of comprehension and commitment. Comprehension continues to increase, and like the incline of a stairway, our commitment is a step-by-step progress—a "yes, Lord, yes, Lord," response to what we understand. You can grow as fast as you want to spiritually.

Emotional differences and moralistic differences are factors in experiences of commitment, depending on the size of the step of faith or change one experiences at a given time. For example, one committing his life to Christ at twelve years of age is not committing to as much total-life change as one who makes such a commitment at twenty-five, with all its related implications. But one commitment is not necessarily more sincere or more meaningful than the other. This accounts for some of the psychological differences in conversion.

Following conversion one may even yet refuse to take a next step in truth. To not go on in the will of Christ when it is known is "carnality," a refusal to obey or to walk in the Spirit. Paul writes to the Romans that to be carnally minded leads to death (Romans 8:13). If one goes on a tangent of self-will, the gap between his comprehension and his commitment will increase. When a person faces this honestly and makes a rededication of his life to Christ, the emotional and/or moral change may be as great or greater than in his original conversion. But the important thing is his surrender to the will of God, not the particular experience-dimensions of his commitment. "The Spirit has given us life; he must also control our lives." (Galatians 5:25.)

God's work in us, by his Word and Spirit, is to bring us to wholeness. How often I have rejoiced in a new spiritual experience only to be humbled by the realization that it exposed other areas of my person that need perfecting. Growth in knowledge introduces us to new areas for our understanding, and thus keeps life from becoming stale and makes our discipleship exciting. True commitment to Christ is never static; it is ever a new discovery of the implications of his Lordship and of his plan. To walk with God is exciting. It frees us from a legalism of religious deed.

6

Happy Are Those Who Show Mercy

Happy are those who show mercy to others: God will show mercy to them! (Matthew 5:7)

The Bible is the expression of one great covenant of grace throughout. The full meaning was not evident until the complete revelation in Christ. The Old Testament refers again and again to God's mercy, to his steadfast love. The New Testament speaks of God's love in Christ—"God loved the world so much that he gave his only Son" (John 3:16). In the writings of the New Testament period the word "grace" comes into the vocabulary as the basic expression of God's mercy. John writes, "God gave the Law through Moses; but grace and truth come through Jesus Christ" (John 1:17).

It is still true that no man has seen God, but we have seen Jesus Christ, and God is like Jesus. In his life we discover how God gives acceptance to us. We see God in action—caring, forgiving, helping, with no thought of something in return. It is this quality of mercy that turns us to the Savior.

All that we have from God is by his grace and mercy. We do not merit or deserve his favor. As disciples we pray in the name of Jesus. This is our confession that it is by the grace we know through Jesus Christ that we approach God. In our identification with Christ we come directly to God in prayer; we have no other mediator. Jesus introduces us to the pattern of prayer with a very simple and direct approach to God.

It should be recognized that if God made it difficult for us to come to him we could justly ask why. What kind of God would make it hard for us to get to him? The good news of the gospel is that God has come to us, that he cares, that he wants us in fellowship. A caring God is the good news of the gospel, a truth that surpasses all impersonal or abstract concepts of God. The uniqueness of the Christian understanding of God is the Christlikeness of God.

Our consciousness of a merciful God undergirds our prayer life.

This is the way you should pray:
"Our Father in heaven:
May your name be kept holy,
May your Kingdom come,
May your will be done on earth as it is in heaven.
Give us today the food we need;
Forgive us the wrongs that we have done,
As we forgive the wrongs that others have done us.

Do not bring us to hard testing, but keep us safe from the Evil One."
[For thine is the kingdom, and the power, and the glory, for ever. Amen. KJV] (Matthew 6:9-13)

Mercy is learned from God, who is the source of mercy. John writes, "Herein is love, not that we loved God, but that He loved us and sent His Son to be the 'expression of mercy' on account of sin" (my own translation). Jesus' basic concept of God, underlying his approach to prayer, is that of God being merciful. We can come to God because he opens himself to us. I have found this to be most meaningful in personal prayer, to know God shares himself with me, that he cares.

Addressing God by the word "thou" rather than "you" is more than archaic English, for "thou" denotes reverence and the singularity of addressing "one." This idea is effectively discussed by Elton Trueblood, who sees the word as one of the most valuable in the biblical heritage. "God is not One who is discusssed or argued about, but One who is encountered." He points out the moving and radical change in Psalm 23 from God being spoken about to the expression where God is spoken to. "At the profoundest depths men talk not *about* God but *with* Him." [1]

The Lord's Prayer is a model in meaning and manner. (1) We approach God in *humility*. We are to come before him as a person, with reverent worship of his name, and with full respect for the priority of his King-

[1] Trueblood, *The New Man for Our Time,* p. 121.

dom. (2) We are to acknowledge God's providence *honestly*. *His* will is to be done. *His* kindness gives us the sustenance of life. *His* pardon frees us. And *his* care helps us in temptation. (3) We are to acclaim God's purpose in *hope*. His Kingdom, his power, and his glory will triumph ultimately. We should learn to pray in this manner, to think of God as a merciful Father, to see his will in our daily lives, to ask his guidance to keep us from situations that solicit us to sin, and to live with his ultimate purpose as our goal.

Prayer is the indication of how aware we are of God's mercy. He is willing to share himself with us if we come to him to meet him. We miss the meaning of prayer if all we do is to treat him like a teller at a bank who hands out what has been put on deposit for us. Mercy makes possible fellowship between two unequals and does so without condescension. This is the basis of our freedom to say, "Our Father."

Our capacity to share
enlarges our capacity to receive.

> For if you forgive others the wrongs they have done you, your Father in heaven will also forgive you. (Matthew 6:14)

A direct relationship exists between our understanding of mercy and our ability to receive mercy. Some persons react against the idea that God's forgiving love at Calvary requires the innocent to suffer for the guilty. But that is exactly the way life is at the interpersonal level.

Forgiveness costs. Meaningful friendships or a successful marriage are impossible unless we forgive each other. In the act of forgiving the hurt we have suffered, we free the one who has hurt us by not holding his transgression against him. This does not mean that we approve of what he has done, but neither does condemning the sin require crushing the sinner. Forgiveness means that the innocent one carries his own indignation on the sin of the guilty one and lets the guilty go free.

When a person sins against you and then asks forgiveness, if you first make him crawl before you and then say he is forgiven, the truth is that you have not really forgiven him. What you did was to punish him emotionally, to balance your emotional ledger, and then say "Now we can forget it." To forgive is actually to free the other person from recrimination or judgment, leaving the door open for the reconciliation and the "healing" of the situation. Such forgiveness means to carry your own anger and disappointment at another's action. Rather than pour out your resentment on him, you let him go free.

This is the meaning of Calvary. Here Christ tasted death for us. He bore the full intensity of our sin in his crucifixion. (I Peter 2:24.) He absorbed our hostility, our rejection, even to death, and still offers forgiveness. Now we are justified freely by his grace, through the forgiveness that is in Christ Jesus.

In this passage of the Sermon on the Mount, Jesus anticipates the full cost of forgiving us, a cost to be experienced at the Cross. But he is asking us to recognize the necessity of our forgiving others if we would enjoy the forgiveness of God who invites all men to share his mercy. Our capacity to share with others enlarges our capacity to receive.

Jesus came to share with man, even though it meant sharing man's hostility all the way to the Cross. Literally he bore our sins in his body on the Cross. He took man's hostility onto himself all the way to death. Having tasted death for every man, he can now absorb the depth of our sin and forgive us. Forgiveness always means absorbing the problem.

Tolstoi one day observed the poor peasants working on his father's estate. Putting on old clothes he went out and joined them in their work. They laughed and joked for awhile, then said, "But this is our lot for life, and you can go back to your royal life whenever you choose." And, of course, he did. In the same way Satan taunted Jesus, saying that he could retreat from the human dilemma. But Jesus didn't leave; he stayed with us in our plight even to his death. He absorbed the full intensity of man's hostility, even to death, and didn't "cop out." Forgiveness involves taking the full brunt of a man's sin, absolving it by not striking back. When one forgives, he helps a sin to die.

Our unwillingness to forgive is a rejection of the expression of God's redeeming grace through us.

But if you do not forgive the wrongs of others, then your Father in heaven will not forgive the wrongs you have done. (Matthew 6:15)

God's work of redeeming man is his primary program in the world. He expresses his grace as willingness to forgive and accept man. But no one can accept that forgiveness and be true to God's grace if he himself will not witness to that forgiveness by extending it to others. This is not legal language; it is a declaration of fact. We are dealing with attitudes in this sermon. One who refuses to express love and forgiveness to others is standing in his own way by this attitude. He is preventing himself from sharing in forgiveness.

Jesus illustrates this in Matthew 18 with the story of the man who owed his master thousands of dollars. The debtor could never keep up paying the interest, let alone the principal. Knowing his master would sell him and his family as slaves to get all he could on the debt, the man went and begged for mercy, and for time to pay what he could. His master was impressed by his spirit and forgave him the debt. Here is the cost of forgiveness: the guilty went free and the innocent carried the loss of the money.

But the servant went out and met a man who owed him a few dollars. He demanded the money and heard the same plea for mercy that he himself had made to his master, but he had no mercy and had the debtor put in jail. When this news came to his master, the only just thing he could do was to condemn the man for his attitude and send him to the prison. So Jesus makes clear that to receive freely of God's forgiveness means sharing the full meaning of that forgiveness, thereby extending God's expression of mercy. "Happy are those who show mercy to others: God will show mercy to them."

> The quality of mercy is not strain'd,
> It droppeth as the gentle rain from heaven
> Upon the place beneath: it is twice bless'd;
> It blesseth him that gives and him that takes:
> 'Tis mightiest in the mightiest; it becomes
> The throned monarch better than his crown;
> His sceptre shows the force of temporal power,
> The attribute to awe and majesty,
> Wherein doth sit the dread and fear of kings;
> But mercy is above the sceptred sway,
> It is enthroned in the hearts of kings,
> It is an attribute to God himself,
> And earthly power doth then show likest God's
> When mercy seasons justice.[2]

There is no freedom like the release of forgiveness. Fellowship and friendship are possible only as we accept each other. This acceptance is to be genuine, not a facade that ignores the guilt problems that separate us. To accept another in grace means that I can have fellowship with him through genuine, loving forgiveness.

In spite of our guilt, God forgives. Loving us, he cares more about us than about what we've done. His act of accepting me "in Christ" causes me to stand in freedom, forgiven.

And one who knows this fellowship will live differently. One who experiences forgiveness at Calvary will never consider sin lightly. To experience forgiveness is to enter freedom.

[2] Shakespeare (*The Merchant of Venice*)

The experience of forgiveness has the power to change one's life. In telling the story of Augustine's conversion, J. B. Meyer's account climaxes with the words: "No further would I read, nor was there need, for instantly all my heart was flooded with a light of peace, all the sadness of doubt melted away." He had found honest release in the awareness of God's forgiveness.

7

Happy Are the Pure in Heart

Happy are the pure in heart: they will see God! (Matthew 5:8)

"Purity of heart," said Kierkegaard, "is to will one will." Our Master emphasizes this in the next passage. Every man faces the basic question, Who is going to be worshiped in my life. The call of Christ is for us to let God be God in our personal lives. It has been said, "The road without God is impossible because you run into the moral law." The truth of the matter is that you run into God himself.

Man's greatest issue is whether he wants God in his life. This is a volitional matter, combining the forces of the emotions and of the mind. The question is not how one thinks about God but how one feels about God. How one feels about another is what determines relationship. The science of psychology has helped us understand that where a person is concerned, the issue becomes one of acceptance or rejection.

Purity of heart means that we are dealing with the center of our motivation, our attitudes and aspirations. This is an inner integrity of spirit, of motive. For too many people purity is more a matter of the body than of the mind and heart. Jesus is calling us to a pure mind and a pure motive. The apostle Paul speaks of this when he says that every thought is to be brought under control of Christ.

This obedience to Christ is not bondage; it is the necessary discipline for freedom in a meaningful pattern of life. The hymn writer expresses this paradox in the lines,

> Make me a captive, Lord,
> And then I shall be free;
> Force me to render up my sword,
> And I shall conqueror be.

Only the disciplined athlete is free to compete in the Olympics. Only the disciplined musician is free to present a recital. Someone once said, "The difference between a river and a swamp is that a river has borders; the swamp has none."

Some of the greatest principles for practical living are found in this section of Jesus' sermon. As to property and wealth Jesus says, "Do not save riches here on earth. . . . Instead save riches in heaven" (Matthew 6:19-20). This defies the materialistic status-seeking that motivates so much of our living and dominates people who find their security in things. This calls us to find security in spiritual values, to learn to share in love. It calls us to be enriched by and to enrich others through interpersonal relations, sharing the joy and peace of Christ.

Further, Jesus says that it is essential that we decide on priorities. A man is a unit, and wholeness means one doesn't have divided loyalties. "You cannot serve both God and money." (Matthew 6:24.) In putting God first, you declare your loyalty and establish priorities for life. As a consequence you are free from worry over petty things and are able to trust him as you give yourself to causes that are major. It is in this light that Jesus offers a clear philosophy for Christian living: "Give first place to his [God's] Kingdom and to what he requires, and he will provide you with all these other things" (Matthew 6:23).

Significantly the emphasis on purity of heart speaks to our *worship,* our *work,* and our *worries.* Ours is to will one will—God's will for us. Worship is the reverence of a total life committed to the will of God. A Christian view of work holds it to be the service which undergirds the personality developing in the will of God. Worry is answered when our trust in God is primary and the cares of life are seen as incidental. Having a pure heart means that I will only God's will. Jesus outlines the implications of this integrity in the next section of his sermon.

The pure in heart move beyond forms to fellowship in the experience of worship.

And when you fast, do not put on a sad face like the show-offs do. They go around with a hungry look so that

> everybody will be sure to see that they are fasting. Remember this! They have already been paid in full. When you do without food, wash your face and comb your hair, so that others cannot know that you are fasting—only your Father, who is unseen, will know. And your Father, who sees what you do in private, will reward you. (Matthew 6:16-18)

In a similar style as his treatment on prayer, Jesus here condemns religious observances that are mere expressions of pious behavior and asks for sincerity and authentic behavior. Fasting is not scheduled by the calendar; nor is it a regular routine to impress others. Fasting is a sincere experience of foregoing some normal satisfactions in life for spiritual renewal and strength. While there are doubtless physical benefits from fasting, in freeing the body for more clarity of mind and spirit, the emphasis here is on the importance of sacrificing legitimate things for spiritual ministries. Jesus' emphasis on motive is basic for spiritual renewal.

Paul admonishes husbands and wives that fasting may also mean temporarily foregoing participation in sex for the sake of involvement in spiritual exercises and meditation. "Do not deny yourselves to each other, unless you first agree to do so for a while, in order to spend your time in prayer; but then resume normal marital relations, so that your lack of self-control will not make you give in to Satan's temptation." (I Corinthians 7:5.) He is careful to point out that too long a period of limitation in this aspect of marital love becomes a hindrance in spiritual freedom.

It is important to have a good balance between the physical and spiritual dimensions of life. Man is a unit, and we don't separate the physical from the spiritual. The Christian faith does not count one more spiritual who withdraws from the physical to live in the realm of mind and spirit. In the biblical perspective, which regards man as a unit, we take the physical realm seriously, seeking to live the Christian faith in a well-ordered life. The Incarnation is the ultimate example that holiness is not a withdrawal from a normal life. The Word became flesh (John 1:14). With this in mind William Temple wrote, "It [Christianity] is the most avowedly materialist of all the great religions." [1]

Humanness and sinfulness are not synonymous. God created a good world. God could become man in the Incarnation without being sinful. We can be disciples and live Christlike lives now in this physical body. Our future is not as an eternally floating mind but in a resurrected body, which means we retain individuality and personality. True piety is participation with Christ in the total of one's life. To worship truly is to reverence God in all of life, in work as well as meditation.

This is expressed in Millet's picture *The Angelus*. The couple close the day's work in the field with prayer. The rays of the evening sun do not fall on the distant church steeple, nor upon the folded hands in prayer, but upon the farm tools, the implements of toil. True reverence brings the total life into a righteous relation with God.

[1] William Temple, *Nature, Man, and God* (New York: St. Martins Press, 1934), p. 478.

The pure in heart live for spiritual rather than material riches.

Do not save riches here on earth, where moths and rust destroy, and robbers break in and steal. Instead, save riches in heaven, where moths and rust cannot destroy, and robbers cannot break in and steal. For your heart will always be where your riches are. The eyes are like a lamp for the body: if your eyes are clear, your whole body will be full of light; but if your eyes are bad, your body will be in darkness. So if the light in you turns out to be darkness, how terribly dark it will be!" (Matthew 6:19-23)

We cannot satisfy our hunger for God with things. Man is basically a spiritual being, living by love, peace, joy, integrity, and friendship, and these dimensions are not fulfilled by material riches. To lay up treasures on earth is to find one's fulfillment in satisfying the desire for power by control over things. To lay up treasure in heaven is to find delight in the things of God's order for life. This is not to say that material things are unimportant but rather that they are servant and not lord. Trueblood says, "The follower of Christ does not ignore or deny the material order, but asserts its reality and understands its subordination." [2] You must master money or money will master you. Where your treasure is, where your priorities are placed, determines the center of your life.

Often the basic areas of temptation for younger people are in physical desires, for middle-aged people in the world of ambition, and for older people in the realm of doubting or feelings of uselessness. Of these, the most

[2] Trueblood, *The New Man for Our Time,* p. 82.

crucial may be the temptations facing middle age. Ambition for material status often dominates a couple's life at the very time when the children need a balanced exposure to spiritual realities as well as to material things. In our affluent society, with money to acquire the things we want, the most acute test of our values is in how we spend our money. Jesus says that we need a clear vision of his priorities, an eye single to his purpose, that the whole of our lives may be enriched.

The pure in heart give absolute commitment to a single Master.

> No one can be a slave to two masters: he will hate one and love the other; he will be loyal to one and despise the other. You cannot serve both God and money.
>
> This is why I tell you: do not be worried about the food and drink you need to stay alive, or about clothes for your body. After all, isn't life worth more than food? and isn't the body worth more than clothes? Look at the birds flying around: they do not plant seeds, gather a harvest, and put it in barns; your Father in heaven takes care of them! Aren't you worth much more than birds? (Matthew 6:14-26)

Purity of heart is to will *one* will. Jesus said, "No man can serve two masters." In a day of divided loyalties, of forces in society which polarize us, this statement is especially demanding. Our choice is between giving priority to the sacred or to the secular. The disciple who gives his loyalty to the sacred will then be able to see the secular in proper perspective.

"Engagement in social struggles does not absolve a

man of the requirements of personal morality." [3] Obedience is first of all, and above all, to God. This is true with respect to all earthly powers—"no authority exists without God's permission"—for the scripture means they are under God and not in the place of God. (Romans 13:1.) There are times when the disciple must say, "We ought to obey God rather than man." We are called to live under the mandate of Christ. The whole of life is to be sanctified by the presence and rule of the Spirit of Christ.

The pure in heart live above anxiety by their pursuit of God.

Which one of you can live a few years more by worrying about it?

And why worry about clothes? Look how the wild flowers grow: they do not work or make clothes for themselves. But I tell you that not even Solomon, as rich as he was, had clothes as beautiful as one of these flowers. It is God who clothes the wild grass—grass that is here today, gone tomorrow, burned up in the oven. Will he not be all the more sure to clothe you? How little is your faith! So do not start worrying: "Where will my food come from? or my drink? or my clothes?" (These are the things the heathen are always after.) Your Father in heaven knows that you need all these things.

Instead, give first place to his Kingdom and to what he requires, and he will provide you with all these other things. So do not worry about tomorrow; it will have enough worries of its own. There is no need to add to the troubles each day brings. (Matthew 6:27-34)

[3] *Ibid.*, p. 91.

Man is prone to worry because as a thinking creature he is able to project into the future. But the answer for tomorrow is trust, not worry, to believe God for tomorrow as well as today. Worry doesn't improve anything anyway. Worry negatively affects the worrier. Worry expends a lot of psychic energy needed for other things. Worry makes one ineffective in the actual demands of life. Above all, worry is irreverent—it is an unconscious attempt to play God, to take over the control of circumstances beyond our control. We must learn to trust, to take seriously both God's providence and his promise to answer prayer.

Jesus' guidance is positive. The central command here is "Give first place to his [God's] Kingdom and to what he requires, and he will provide you will all these things." This is not an escapism; it is not ignoring the problem. This calls us to begin at the right place. That is, by involving ourselves in seeking God's best, other things will then be conditioned in our lives appropriately.

Jesus closes this section with some very practical advice. Leave tomorrow to tomorrow; there is enough in each day for one to face it in faith and victory. The evidence of trusting God is in our ability to face things as they come, drawing on his grace. Consider some of our follies. We read books about relating to people yet isolate ourselves from our families. We talk of the importance of victorious living yet fail to keep up in today's meditation and prayer.

"Happy are the pure in heart: they will see God!" The beatific vision, the awareness of God, is missed when our motives are wrong. When the heart is impure, it is not God that we see, but the rationalizations or defenses we've created for the impurity. Jesus' own version of God was clear because he always sought the will of God above all else. One can see God clearly if his heart is pure.

This fidelity to Chirst is not a legalism of Christian morality but a relationship to the Person of Christ, which makes this a personal discipleship. And discipleship itself is a matter of spirit, not a code of moralism. One of the fine expressions of this truth comes from the sixteenth century Free-Church exponent, Michael Sattler.[4]

TWO KINDS OF OBEDIENCE

> Obedience is of two kinds, servile and filial. The filial has its source in the love of the Father; . . . the servile . . . in a love of reward or of oneself. The filial is never able to do enough for Him; but he who renders servile obedience thinks he is constantly doing too much for Him. The filial rejoices in the chastisement of the Father although he may not have transgressed in anything; the servile wishes to be without chastisement although he may do nothing right.
>
> The filial has its treasure and righteousness in the Father; . . . the servile person's treasure and piety are the works which he does in order to be pious. The filial remains in the house and inherits all the Father has; the servile wishes to reject this and receive his lawful (*gesatzten*) reward. The servile looks to the external;

[4] For an easy introduction to Michael Sattler, his beliefs, his work, and his martyrdom in 1527, read my historical novel, *Pilgrim Aflame* (Scottsdale, Pa.: Herald Press, 1967).

. . . the filial is concerned about the inner witness and the Spirit. The servile is imperfect and therefore his Lord finds no pleasure in him; the filial strives for and attains perfection, and . . . the Father cannot reject him.

The filial is not contrary to the servile, as it might appear, but is better and higher. And therefore let him who is servile seek for the better, the filial; he dare not be servile at all.[5]

[5] Translated by John C. Wenger, in *Mennonite Quarterly Review,* January, 1947, with critical notes.

8

Happy Are Those Who Work for Peace

Happy are those who work for peace among men: God will call them his sons! (Matthew 5:9)

Human nature seems to be inclined toward piece-making instead of peacemaking. We divide into pieces instead of bringing divisions together in unity. All of us have a tendency to be sure our opinions are right, and often insist on them at the expense of good relations with others. To use an old adage, some drive the nail so hard they split the board. Ours is a *ministry* and a *message* of reconciliation (II Corinthians 5:18-19). As ambassadors for Christ we must be certain that we also have a manner of reconciliation.

A peacemaker knows how to play down differences so that people can actually hear each other. A peacemaker is honest, but he doesn't, in his honesty, try to cover every aspect of an issue and simply add confusion to the situation. A peacemaker is fair; he does not work by underhanded digs or insinuations. His concerns or criticisms are shared where they will do some good, and he does not work by anonymous means.

A pastor once received a critical note anonymously. He said nothing about it to anyone. Months later, while he was working with men of his church in remodeling their building for worship, one of the men said, "Pastor, I understand that some months ago you received a very critical note, and I want to let you know we appreciate you and have confidence in you." The pastor said, "Ssh, don't tell anyone—we're the only two people that know of it!"

To be a peacemaker means that we learn to minimize problems and maximize programs. Many problems will work themselves out if instead of concentrating on them we concentrate on constructive matters.

But problems do not disappear by ignoring them. Some persist even though we work constructively at corrective measures. The solution of a problem depends more often than not on the spirit in which you work at it rather than on the answers offered.

Seeking the counsel of others in major problems will often serve to help a person analyze and distinguish answers for himself. As counselors we serve as reference agents. We achieve our goal when we help the seeker find the answer for himself. Such is the role of a peacemaker. To serve in this way there are certain guides we need to accept.

A peacemaker has learned to be honest before ultimate judgment.

> Do not judge others, so that God will not judge you—because God will judge you in the same way you judge others, and he will apply to you the same rules you apply to others. (Matthew 7:1-2)

Jesus' teaching about judgment is not to remove it but to show us its implications. Christ himself judged and showed us how to be men who are both tough and tender. The implication of Christ's teaching is that judgment involves self-judgment. Paul Tillich makes this point remarkably clear in his emphasis on new men for our age.[1] We can be both tough and tender when we honestly discipline ourselves before we react to others.

Everything you and I have done today stands ultimately under the judgment of God. We are eternally the persons who have done what we have done. When this is clear in our minds we will be less prone to be judgmental of others and will instead judge ourselves. Even our judgmental attitude stands under God's ultimate judgment. James writes, "Who do you think you are, to judge your fellow man?" (James 4:12).

Here again Jesus makes clear that the way we relate to others is an indication of the way we interpret God's relating to us. On the human level this is also the law of life; we receive in similar fashion as we give. If one would have friends he must be friendly. Smile and men will smile

[1] Paul Tillich, *The New Being* (New York: Scribner's, 1955), p. 4.

back. Raise your voice in anger and another will tend to raise his in response. Believe in people and trust them, and they will tend to behave accordingly. Be judgmental of others and play god over them, and God will meet you on your own ground with his judgment. "A man will reap exactly what he plants" (Galatians 6:7).

A peacemaker has learned to be fair in his criticisms.

> Why, then, do you look at the speck in your brother's eye, and pay no attention to the log in your own eye? How dare you say to your brother, "Please, let me take that speck out of your eye," when you have a log in your own eye? You impostor! Take the log out of your own eye first, and then you will be able to see and take the speck out of your brother's eye. (Matthew 7:3-5)

We do not close our eyes to the faults and sins about us. If we take sin seriously in our lives, we will take it seriously in others. But often we excuse ourselves and rationalize our sins while we are severe on others.

Jesus illustrates our hypocrisy by a bit of humorous ridicule. He pictures us in our phoniness offering to pick a speck of dust from our brother's eye while a log is protruding from our own. Beyond the tendency we have to notice our brother's faults and excuse our own is a question, why do we recognize a particular fault so readily in our brother? Psychologically our criticism of another is often a projection of our own problem. There are doubtless other faults in an individual besides the one that impresses us. Our selection of the particular one may be a projection of our own self-consciousness about this problem.

To be a peacemaker means to be honest in our judgments, to be able to demonstrate that first of all we've criticized and corrected ourselves. If we are sincere about correcting and improving life, we demonstrate it by our total spirit and behavior. This is the disciple's attitude toward himself—correcting and enriching his own life to contribute to others. Some of us really don't want to be corrected. We rather enjoy our problems, enjoy calling attention to ourselves like the hypochondriac who had written on his tombstone. "Now will you believe that I'm sick?"

A peacemaker has learned to use discretion in dealing with men.

> Do not give what is holy to dogs—they will only turn and attack you; do not throw your pearls in front of pigs—they will only trample them underfoot. (Matthew 7:6)

Jesus' striking word-picture of casting pearls before swine emphasizes the folly of acting indiscriminately. Peacemaking is a most difficult work. We are to use discretion in dealing with people or we will only suffer for getting involved. Good peacemaking advice given at the wrong time may not only be rejected but may call forth hostility. We need to use discernment in grappling with difficulties.

By using discretion I have frequently realized that the

Spirit of God is likewise at work in others, that a bit of time removes one from the emotional heat of the issue and provides for more objectivity. The peacemaker is the Holy Spirit, and we must learn to be sensitive to him.

Whether it be at the personal, social, or national level, peacemaking is never easy. It cannot be achieved simply by offering good advice to strangers. There must be the development of trust, of confidence in one another. Only when I am sure of another's good motives will I meet him halfway.

Often a neutral party can be the agent of reconciliation. By helping interpret one person to another he is often able to establish an element of trust that can bring peace.

Paul writes regarding our personal peace with others, "Do everything possible, on your part, to live at peace with all men" (Romans 12:18). For someone who knows Christ and his Spirit working within him, there is a greater potential for making peace than he often recognizes.

Our attitude toward others is the evidence of how sincerely we love people. Since God's ultimate work is redeeming people, our attitude toward others shows how much we love God and his work. No one lies outside the circle of God's concern. God loves all men. Christ died to redeem all men. The Spirit wants to use us to evangelize all men.

Our commission is to go into the world and preach the gospel to every person. There is no one for whom Christ died that we are exempt from seeking to win to Christ. We cannot call a man an enemy and close him out any more than Jesus closed out his enemies at the Cross. "Forgive them, Father! they don't know what they are doing." (Luke 23:34.) He made peace through the gift of his life. Peacemaking becomes the pattern of evangelism—winning men through giving ourselves for them so that we may introduce them to Christ.

Blessed are the peacemakers; they shall be known as children of God. I recall, as a boy, my father working on a construction job in an apartment complex. After some months he was promoted to foreman, a position another man wanted. For days this man tried various things to turn the men against my father. A part of this was to ridicule some of my father's Christian convictions, especially his commitment to the way of peace and nonviolence.

Suddenly a slump in work meant that a number of men were laid off, including my father's rival. For a number of days following, when my father went to work, he'd see this man among those at the gate hoping to be given work.

One day there was need for two more men on one of the jobs and my father went to the gate to pick two. He looked over the crowd and picked the first carpenter and told him to go to work; then, looking over the rest, he picked out his rival and said, "Get your tools, Bob, and come to work."

Years later I was back in that city in an evangelistic preaching mission. One night a man came forward at the close of the service and asked me if I knew C. A. Augsburger. When I replied that he was my father, he responded, "Now, there's a man who lives for God! I saw it in his attitude at work." The thing that brought that man to hear the gospel was not my preaching, but the example of my father, whose commitment to Christ made him a peacemaker.

9

Happy Are Those Who Suffer Persecution

Happy are those who suffer persecution because they do what God requires: the Kingdom of heaven belongs to them! (Matthew 5:10)

Persecution arises because someone dares to be different. We are so inclined to live by the status quo that a different way of life scares us. While it hurts to be different, that is exactly where the strength of the faith is found. To follow Christ is to go against the stream of humanity, to live by another directive.

As a teen-ager I committed my life to the lordship of Christ, and, while very imperfectly, I sought to live as a disciple. In public high school this meant declining practices some of my associates followed. Peer-group pressure is hard to face, yet obedience to Christ has its own rewards. The more difficult persecution to bear gracefully is that which comes when we've done something good. When we've done wrong the persecution complements our feeling of needing correction. But to try to help someone and be rebuffed is very hard to accept.

Jesus knew what this meant. "He came to his own country, but his own people did not receive him." (John 1:11.) When he was on the Cross, they were not satisfied with crushing his body; they tried to crush his spirit as well. They taunted him, "He saved others but he can't save himself."

The ability to accept persecution for righteousness' sake is in direct proportion to one's awareness of belonging to the Kingdom of heaven. When you are thoroughly convinced of the validity of a cause, you can endure persecution for the sake of your ultimate goal.

For over fifteen years I have worked in evangelistic preaching missions often referred to as "mass evangelism crusades." These have taken me to many cities of America, and around the world several times. The conviction for this work on an interchurch basis came to me from the Spirit of God, in spite of my rural conservative background, and in spite of being from a smaller denomination with its unique commitments to discipleship and pacifism. Often misunderstood from within my brotherhood for my work with other groups, from beyond my brotherhood for differences of perspective, I have needed to learn from the Spirit not to be defensive. There is a freedom in learning to obey God and leave the rest with him.

Jesus is speaking of persecution for righteousness' sake, and we need to be certain about what this righteousness is. Earlier in his sermon he said we need a righteousness superior to that of the scribes and Pharisees.

In Jesus' ministry he brought a higher morality—a new morality—to man. He elevated the person above the code. He elevated love above perfunctory observance. For example, when men brought to Jesus a woman taken in adultery and asked him what to do in view of Moses' law, Jesus answered by introducing them to a higher law —the value of a person. Theirs was a code to judge men by, a negative evaluation of man's direction. His was a righteousness that could turn her to the right way and save her life—"Leave," he said, "but do not sin again" (John 8:7).

Those living righteously have found the dynamic of communion with God.

> Ask, and you will receive; seek, and you will find; knock, and the door will be opened to you. For everyone who asks will receive, and he who seeks will find, and the door will be opened to him who knocks. Would any one of you fathers give his son a stone, when he asks you for bread? Or would you give him a snake, when he asks you for fish? As bad as you are, you know how to give good things to your children. How much more, then, your Father in heaven will give good things to those who ask him! (Matthew 7:7-11)

This is where righteousness begins—with a right relation to God himself. We come directly to him as a son to his father. Jesus expresses the formula for this relationship with an invisible God very simply, "Ask, and you will receive." Our relationship with God is one of partnership, one of sharing. We do not practice religion to win his approval; we participate with him in carrying out his work in the world.

This passage also suggests that God is not difficult to get to. As a father meets his son on the basis of concern and love, so we can count on God reaching out to us to be a Father. And as a Father he has manifested his will for us in his Son. Through the centuries and in various cultures, men and women have demonstrated that the means of growth in the life of the Spirit is in contemplation on Christ. Elton Trueblood says, "The more deeply an honest man concentrates his attention upon Christ, the more he comes to the conclusion that the momentous possibility is an actuality." [1]

The basic manner in which the Church affects the social order around it is through its members. The Church is its members; it is people, not a building, and as the people of God engaged in secular occupations it influences society for God. Christopher Dawson says, "Individual acts of spiritual decision ultimately bear social fruit." [2] Paul writes, "You yourselves are the letter we have, . . . for everyone to know and read" (II Corinthians 3:2). We stand effectively before men because we stand expectantly before God.

[1] *The New Man for Our Time,* p. 76.

[2] Christopher Dawson, *The Historic Reality of Christian Culture* (New York: Harper, 1960), p. 18.

Those living righteously practice the good they wish to see in others.

Do for others what you want them to do for you: this is the meaning of the Law of Moses and the teaching of the prophets. (Matthew 7:12)

This statement is the motto for positive Christian action. It is built on the passage immediately preceding. God practices the good toward us that he wants to see in us. This is a basic principle of the psychology of good relationships. Now he asks us to become engaged in positive action, to do to others what we'd like to see from them. This means taking the initiative in the promotion of good.

It has been my privilege to work with scores of denominations in preaching missions. I'm sure that no one group has captured the Kingdom! We need to hear each other and be enriched by each other. The contribution we wish to make to another will be received best when our behavior manifests love and respect.

The ideals we hold are to be demonstrated rather than demanded. Holiness is propagated not by words but by example. We need to realize the tremendous influence a Christlike life can have on others. The world has enough scholars and leaders; what it needs is more everyday saints.

It is important that we rediscover a basically religious approach to social issues. This is where the evangelical gospel has its greatest strength. We need to recognize that the problem of racial antagonism is basically religious. To the honest researcher, it is abundantly evident that the lasting contributions to racial equality have been made by religious men. Anyone who has read from the *Journal* of John Woolman of the eighteenth century or the writings of Martin Luther King of the twentieth is well aware of this. It is the same with other social issues. It is the Christian conviction of the sacredness of persons that motivates us in Christian social action. When we see every man as God's handiwork and likewise every man equally as under God's judgment, we are called to a social order of equal opportunity and justice. This awareness, coupled with Christian compassion, is the most revolutionary or transforming force for any society.

Those living righteously live daily in the light of life's basic commitment.

> Go in through the narrow gate, for the gate is wide and the road is easy that leads to hell, and there are many who travel it. The gate is narrow and the way is hard that leads to life, and few people find it. (Matthew 7:13-14)

All of life takes its direction from our basic decision to follow Christ. Once we have committed ourselves to follow Christ, the question at the point of decision should not be, will I do the will of God? but rather, what is the will of God? Before our conversion the choice is between the good and the bad, but once we have been converted the choice is between the good, the better, and the best. My choices express my real standard of life—my basic value system.

As president of a Christian college I am convinced

that this awareness of the priority of Christ makes a difference in education. We are educating for a style of life—that of a disciple—not simply to stimulate the quest for knowledge. Furthermore, we aim at student's will, not just at his mind. We seek to promote a Christian world view which expresses the matter of commitment to the lordship of Christ in relation to our fellow man in a way that both recognizes the sacredness of life and seeks to influence others to become our brothers in Christ.

Truth is power, for it is God's truth, calling persons to wholeness and thereby leading us to true happiness. The word Jesus uses in the Beatitudes for blessed means happy or joyful. One may get pleasure from things, but we only find joy in relationships.

The decision to commit one's self to another is an expression of faith. Many people fail in this because they have trouble making decisions. Often this is caused by fear of the unknown, fear of the consequences. It is most often due to not having made the basic decision from which other decisions get their direction. One who can't make decisions is saying that basic direction isn't clear. A lady seeing a psychiatrist for some weeks was asked by the doctor, "Do you have trouble making decisions?" To which she replied, "Well, yes and no!"

Jesus calls us to enter the strait gate, the singular way of following the will of God. This is our choice and our privilege. All of life is selective. One can't do everything; he is forced to select. Those selections express one's true self. The sinner who chooses the broad road has chosen to give up the good things on the narrow way, just as definitely as the person who chooses the narrow way has chosen to give up the things on the broad way. When a sinner suggests that the Christian is missing a lot in life, the Christian should remind him of what he is missing!

A friend once asked me if I had ever seen a painting depicting the broad and narrow ways. When I said yes, he asked me to describe it. As I described the painting with the broad road leading down filled with people and the narrow road over at the edge of the picture winding up a mountain to the golden city in the distance, he interrupted. "But that is wrong," he said. "The narrow road is right in the middle of the broad road—just heading the other way."

And that is the way it is. The broad road is the stream of humanity with its back turned toward God, and the narrow road is right in the middle of that stream, just going the other direction.

This is the reason Jesus blesses those persecuted for righteousness' sake. As we walk with him among our fellows, our lives witness to right relation with God. We do this in partnership with God, not by ourselves.

Jesus said, "You can do nothing without me." He comes to us by the Holy Spirit to be a transforming power within us. Of this he said, "If I go away, then I will send him [the Helper] to you" (John 16:7).

Christ is now our representative before the Father, and the Holy Spirit is his representative with us. He shares what can be called "resurrection power" with us, to live above the death-dealing influence of sin. In addition to working *within us,* Jesus listed three things the Spirit is come to do *through us,* making us witnesses of righteousness (John 16:8-11).

First, he convinces the world of the sin of unbelief by our belief in Christ. Second, he convinces the world of unrightousness. While Jesus has gone to the Father and is seen no more, the world sees his righteousness in us. And third, he convinces the world "about judgment, because the ruler of this world has already been judged." That is, people see our freedom and victory over the demonic forces and are thereby reminded that the devil is defeated. The ultimate work of the Spirit is expressed in Jesus' words, "He will give me glory, for he will take what I have to say and tell it to you" (John 16:14).

As disciples, our everyday concern is to be known for righteous living. But this is not to be construed into perfectionism. As Trueblood says, "Perfection is harmful when the abstract best becomes the enemy of the concrete good." [3] We do not operate with a false hope for Utopia. As realists we work to achieve a relative improvement.

Likewise we do not concentrate on persecution or we might stoop to simply being different. In analyzing many differences of Christians from others in society, it may be said this is not what Jesus died to achieve. Men have a deceptive pride in being different. I am personally different in my life-style from many about me—in behavior and in appearance. But the important thing is to know the power of Christ, to be Christlike in spirit. He died to make us new, to make us free to be Christlike.

[3] *The New Man for Our Time,* p. 100.

Our suffering rejection should not be because we are odd, but if it comes, it should come because we represent the Christ whom many reject. Our mission is to build bridges of understanding. We are ambassadors for Christ. To win men is not done by glorying in our being different, but is done by showing the difference between the human will and the way of Christ. This quality of honesty in witness will serve to make faith in Christ clear. As Christian faith is thus understood, commitment to the risen Christ will become an option for our contemporaries.

10

Happy Are Those Who Are Insulted

Happy are you when men insult you . . . because you are my followers. (Matthew 5:11-12)

Submission to Christ and the practice of Christian ethics relate as cause and effect. The cause is relating to Christ as Master; the effect is the fruit of righteousness in one's life. In Romans 6, Paul writes of the experience of surrender to Christ, saying that we "are the slaves of God" (Romans 6:22).

Man's tendency is to maximize the code of conduct rather than the spirit and principles of behavior. Consequently many scholars want to reduce the Christian faith to a system of ethics, to dimensions of thought and life which they can master. This is more comfortable than living by the personalism of relating one's self to a Person. Relating to Christ as Master is discomfiting because our security is in him, not in an achievement of mastery in particular areas. Likewise our witness is to be of him, not a declaration of a position we hold.

When Christian faith is considered as a system of ethics, it can be compared, favorably or unfavorably, with the ethical systems of the other world religions. In such comparison there is repeated emphasis on the moral values Jesus brought. Nevertheless, the importance of Christianity is missed. The person and claims of Christ himself are minimized. Jesus is regarded as a good example for proper behavior but ignored as the One who overcomes our sin of rebellion against God and reconciles us to him.

If we separate ethics from living obedience in the Spirit of Christ, we have only a code of morality. When discipleship is divorced from the inner life of the Spirit it becomes a cold, harsh, legalistic moralism. The emphasis on a life of service must be accompanied by deep inner devotion and a discerning spirit. The value and dynamic of Christian ethics are in the power Christ gives us to live righteously. This power is an energizing for wholeness and love which he brings into the believer's life.

The Spirit of Christ equips us to do the work of evangelism. We must avoid the danger of replacing evangelism with service. The tendency today to reduce evangelism to a program of social action is to pervert and lose one of the most basic aspects of discipleship. Christ called us to "make . . . disciples" (Matthew 28:19), to "catch men" (Mark 1:17), just as clearly as he called us to feed the hungry. We seek to change men and thereby we can change the society. We are here to bring men to God.

One who comes in faith accepts not just a part of Jesus. Accepting the whole Jesus means yielding to his will as Master. But this is in grace, for he not only taught us a new way of life—he offered life. Jesus brings us to God, saying, "Now that you have known me, you will know my Father also." Again he said, "I am the way, I am the truth, I am the life; no one goes to the Father except by me" (John 14:6). And again, "If you do not eat the flesh of the Son of Man and drink his blood you will not have life in yourselves" (John 6:53). The gospel is not offering good advice; it is introducing people to the fellowship of God in Christ, that they may be reconciled to a new life in him.

There are only two types of religion in the world. One type, in which man is reaching out to find God, includes Hinduism and Buddhism; the other is the one in which God has reached down to us. The unique and daring claim of Christian faith is that Jesus Christ is God! Paul says, "It was by God's own decision that the Son has in himself the full nature of God" (Colossians 1:19). And this is where the real point of tension rests. Men can accept the teaching of Jesus for ideals of behavior, but they find it difficult to accept Jesus Christ himself as King of kings and Lord of lords.

In our day, with more interchange between the various religions of the world, this issue of faith becomes more crucial to the life of the Church. The ethical concerns upon which we dialogue must not eclipse the Son himself.

The center of Christian faith is the person of Christ in whom we meet God.

If Jesus Christ was not God come to us, then we would still be without a full revelation. But this is quite inconceivable. We could hardly believe in a God of goodness and love who would let the world exist forever without a full revelation of himself. Nor would we expect God to wait until this late stage of history to communicate with the world. Nor would we expect his disclosure to be other than in the highest form of the world as we know it—the human personality itself. As William Temple wrote: "It would be strange if He acted only in the inorganic and non-spiritual, and dealt with spirits akin to Himself only by the indirect testimony of the rest of His creation." [1] The Scriptures reveal God acting in history—a revelation in the stream of history, preparing man to understand him when he came in Christ. The Bible says, "When the right time finally came, God sent his own Son" (Galatians 4:4). And again, in the last days of the unfolding of God's self-disclosure, "He has spoken to us through his Son . . . the one whom God has chosen to possess all things at the end. He shines with the brightness of God's glory; he is the exact likeness of God's own being. . . . After he had made men clean from their sins, he sat down in heaven at the right side of God" (Hebrews 1:2-3).

The passage from Matthew which expands this beatitude expresses its climactic judgment in the words, "I never knew you" (Matthew 7:23). This is the key issue, whether we know and are known by Christ.

[1] *Nature, Man, and God,* p. 318.

The story of the Christian faith reveals that men who stood for Christ, rather than mere Christianity, were persecuted. In the past religious people, who thought themselves Christians, have been deeply hostile and vicious in antagonism toward other Christians. Witness the Inquisition, the martyrdoms of the sixteenth-century Reformation when both Catholic and Protestant killed Anabaptists. Consider the tensions that arise when a denominational hierarchy feels threatened by a religious revival. The God who shatters idols often works to shatter the religious idols of our institutions, of our structures, even of our symbols of faith. You cannot popularize Jesus Christ—he is divisive. He said in this respect, "I did not come to bring peace, but a sword. . . . A man's worst enemies will be the members of his own family" (Matthew 10:34-36).

But Jesus' words do not concentrate on persecution but on the characteristics of a life lived for Christ's sake. In the final test we do what we do as believers, not because of what others ask or expect, nor even because of loyalty to a pattern, but for Christ's sake.

One living for Christ's sake
can be known by the fruit of his life.

> Watch out for false prophets; they come to you looking like sheep on the outside, but they are really like wild wolves on the inside. You will know them by the way they act. Thorn bushes do not bear grapes, and briars do not bear figs. A healthy tree bears good fruit, while a poor tree bears bad fruit. A healthy tree cannot bear bad fruit, and a poor tree cannot bear good fruit. Any tree that does not bear good fruit is cut down and thrown in the fire.

So, then, you will know the false prophets by the way they act. (Matthew 7:15-20)

Where there is no fruit, there is no living faith. Martin Luther once said, "Just as it is natural for a tree to bear fruit so it is natural for faith to have works." This is what the book of James is all about. The writer emphasizes that the quality of Christian deeds in a person's life is the justification for the claim that he is living in faith.

The true gospel condemns those whose lives do not express Christ. Many are like Simon Magus, who wanted the power of God for selfish advantage rather than for the transformation of the self. He was denounced by Peter as being against Christ because he wanted to use Christ for his own ends. Paul warned the Galatians about those who preach "another gospel" which is not the true gospel.

Jesus' teaching is embarrassing to those who use religion for their advantage but who do not truly serve Christ. Confronting them with the claims of Christ often results in persecution, antagonism, hostility, and ridicule. This persecution is often exercised as an intellectual rejection, a condescending attitude, a sophisticated superiority that looks at those witnessing to simple faith in Christ as naïve. There is often the inference that Christian dedication is a phase in a person's development and that a mature person outgrows it. Keith Miller points out the danger of losing meaningful relation with Christ by listening to psychologists who dismiss relation to God by the inference that the mature man internalizes God, and God is only a symbol as one lives by his mature achievements! But Miller answers as a psychologist by showing our deep, built-in needs for God if we are to know wholeness.[2]

In the final analysis it is not by words but by the fruit of my life that it will become clear where I stand. We must look at our lives, our influence upon our friends, our expression of faith through our families, our patterns of business, and our associations with others to see how genuinely faith is expressed. A true witness discerns evil and warns against ultimate ruin. You can't live for Christ without embarrassing some good people who feel they are adequate without him.

One living for Christ's sake
lives by the will of the Father.

> Not every person who calls me "Lord, Lord," will enter into the Kingdom of heaven, but only those who do what my Father in heaven wants them to do. (Matthew 7:21)

The gospel distinguishes between professing Christ and obeying Christ. Jesus said, "If you obey my teaching you are really my disciples" (John 8:31). John writes, "If we obey God's commands, then we are sure that we know him" (I John 2:3). And this commandment is to "believe on the name of his Son Jesus Christ and love one another, just as Christ commanded us" (I John 3:23).

We make a commitment when we pray the prayer Jesus taught us to pray as we ask, "May your will be done on

[2] *The Second Touch*, p. 67.

earth as it is in heaven." This prayer can only be fulfilled as he begins his work in us. Here we surrender ourselves to the will of the Father. This gives us a perspective for life and offers priorities for action.

God wants the world reconciled to himself. He wants this to start with me, with you. He wants us to live in love and fellowship.

He asks for a sense of global community, with the removal of status barriers and power struggles. He desires to see people enjoy each other rather than things. He expects us to work at correcting social ills. His purpose for each of us today is to enjoy life in his will.

But this passage has in it a note of judgment, of discernment and distinction. "Not every person who says 'Lord, Lord,' will enter into the Kingdom of heaven." In another passage Jesus says, "Many are called, but few are chosen" (Matthew 20:16 KJV). Many are invited in grace, but few are those who sincerely enter God's grace. Many stand outside the circle of fellowship with him and only imitate the good life.

The most subtle idols are those religious forms or doctrinal positions which stop short of the will of God and yet give persons the satisfaction of thinking they are walking with God.

In so-called Christian America, "sacred cows" silence our consciences on the full will of God. We are much too guilty of identifying Christianity with nationalistic Americanism. We thus rob the world of a clear choice for Jesus Christ. But one who points this out and calls for repentance will suffer the persecution of rejection by those who don't want to be disturbed while they keep calling, "Lord, Lord." This comes both from rightists who do not want to recognize the supremacy of the universal Kingdom of Christ, and from leftists who will not recognize the lordship of Christ in their call for social change. A true disciple has to be something of a liberal in being adaptable to the new age and at the same time a conservative in holding to the values verified by the past. This means that he must live uncomfortably with both extremes while seeking to obey Christ.

One who lives for Christ's sake follows the person of Christ as well as the principles of Christ.

> When that Day comes, many will say to me, "Lord, Lord! In your name we told God's message, by your name we drove out many demons and performed many miracles!" Then I will say to them, "I never knew you, Away from me, you evildoers!" (Matthew 7:22-23)

There is a difference between working for Christ and walking with Christ. Some are guilty of a kind of spiritual plagiarism in borrowing teachings from Christ but not accepting him. In American society people can live on the benefits of Christian influence from the past in thought and life, and at the same time reject Christ. The average American agnostic is basically dishonest on this matter. He would need, if he were to be strictly honest, to divest himself of all the advantages in his life which are derived from Christian influence and live totally apart from it to be a true doubter of the significance of Christ.

But this is impossible even if a person switched to an

alternate religion. Later religious thinkers or philosophers have been influenced even in their reactions and defenses by Christianity. Various world religions have added dimensions of faith stimulated by Christian influence.

Can we be honest then? To a significant degree, we can when we admit our biases and work from there. That is why it is more honest to accept the biblical classifications of believer and unbeliever. With this stance we can come to the position where we say, "I do have faith [believe] but not enough. Help me!" (Mark 9:24).

From this position we discover that there are aspects of belief and unbelief in most people. There is not always a clear line between faith and nonfaith. The call of Christ lets us look at the evidence for belief and unbelief and choose to follow him without final answers. He is our answer for faith, the evidence of God's love and grace.

No matter how successful a life may be by the measure of men, its true quality is measured by God. If our lives are impressive but empty, it will show up at the judgment. A boy observed a larger-than-average man stepping on a scales. The instrument wasn't working properly and registered only seventy pounds. As the boy's curiosity got the best of him, he looked around him at the meter. Seeing the low weight he said, "Well, what do you know! He's hollow!"

Let us beware of being "hollow men." Jesus says men will even prophesy or teach in his name, quote his teachings as the greatest, cast out the demonic by the liberating influence of his contribution to the stream of history, but never acknowledge Christ himself.

Jesus stands today as the ultimate expression of truth—about God, about man, about life, about death—but men pass him by. Jesus stands as the Prince of Peace—between man and God, between man and man, and between man and his environment—but men pass him by. Our works in understanding his creation are wonderful, both in the advance of the behavioral sciences and the natural sciences, but we pass him by. In fact, to advance by his insight but stand against him, to use his blessings to get men to trust in our achievements but reject him, is the ultimate treason. His judgment is simple and clear—"I never knew you. Away from me."

We are not going to be judged by one who doesn't understand us. The Bible says, "Our high priest is not one who cannot feel sympathy with our weaknesses. On the contrary, we have a high priest who was tempted in every way that we are, but did not sin" (Hebrews 4:15).

Christ has gone through what we face before us, and coming through it victoriously he extends his hand of love to us. John writes, "There is no fear in love; perfect love drives out all fear" (I John 4:18).

The final judgment is on the basis of man's own choice. Heaven is God's presence, and all will be there who want to be with God as he is known in Christ. Hell is to be away from God, and all will go there who don't want to be with God. In fact, it is God's love that makes hell a necessity.

God doesn't violate man's freedom to reject him. God doesn't coerce a man to respond affirmatively. His love respects the person's freedom to accept or reject his grace. God's love and God's wrath are two sides of the same coin. In love God respects man's freedom to say "no" to him, but without approving it. God's wrath is his exposure of our sin in exercising our freedom negatively, his disapproval of our rejecting him even while he permits it.

The disciple shares God's wrath on sin. If we feel deeply about evil we cannot but be concerned about social evil. But to care about the problems of evil is best expressed by positive correction. The strength of Christian faith is our confession of Christ. Herein lie the principles to correct the perversions in society. Herein lies the power for aggressive evangelism, a witness to the lordship of the risen Christ. What a contrast to the empty quest all about us to find life. Only when we are found of Christ do we find life.

What is tomorrow if you can't see through the maze,
Of belching smoke and stinking gas,
Frivolous escapes from reality,
With sounds of hurry and of fear,
And selfish struggles for power,
With sensual stimulations covering our emptiness?

Where is joy, when life is seen through haze of tears,
That drop upon an unresponsive earth,
With pain from violence and war,
Tensions that tear men's souls apart,
Dividing East from West, and black from white,
Not recognizing men as men?

Where is freedom when man's soul is bound,
And deep within is haze of thought,
With conscience lost amidst peer pressures,

And reason's paths but tangents from the way,
Even God is but a value that men use,
With faith blind hope alone?

What is love when dragged through dirt,
Emptied of soul,
Lost amidst pursuit of things,
Identified with sensual lust,
Made into empty words that isolate persons,
Missing God's purpose for us all,
While we talk of hope, of freedom, and of joy?

11
The Disciples' Approach to the Scriptures

So then, everyone who hears these words of mine and obeys them will be like a wise man who built his house on the rock. The rain poured down, the rivers flooded over, and the winds blew hard against that house. But it did not fall, because it had been built on the rock. Everyone who hears these words of mine and does not obey them will be like a foolish man who built his house on the sand. The rain poured down, the rivers flooded over, the winds blew hard against that house, and it fell. What a terrible fall that was!

Jesus finished saying these things, and the crowds were amazed at the way he taught. He wasn't like their teachers of the Law; instead, he taught with authority. (Matthew 7:24-29)

It is not what the Bible says that divides us, but what we bring to the Bible. If we will let the Bible be its own authority, it will conform our thinking to the mind of Christ. It does little good to confess that we believe in the supreme authority of the Scriptures, then cut them up by our schemes of interpretation. Nor is it honest to say we will read the Bible as literature and not discuss its meaning lest we be sectarian. When we study literature we ask questions about what the author is saying to us.

Often people spend a lot of time talking about the Bible but do not come to the Bible to let it speak for itself. This is inexcusable, for any research that is valid will seek to get to the primary sources. If we are really biblicists we will say, "Show it to me in the Scriptures!" We need to rediscover the truth that what people believe largely determines what they do. We cannot maintain the expression of discipleship if the understanding is inadequate. Our hope for the future lies in renewed convictions, not in new activities.

Persons who regard Christian faith only as a philosophy or a system of ethics ask, "Why the old writings, why the Bible; have we not advanced in understanding the meaning of events in history"? But all such advance does not remove us from giving the primary sources the singular place of authority! Since Christian faith is faith in Christ, and discipleship is following Christ, the Word of the Scriptures stands as the one infallible source for the knowledge of God and the one authoritative Word of faith. Paul writes, "Faith comes from hearing the message" (Romans 10:17).

Faith has the basic meaning of trust, of identification. In fact Eugene Nida, of the American Bible Society, has said that in translating the Bible into another language, when you translate the word "faith" you use the idea or word for "obedience." In Paul's letter to the Romans he says, "He who is righteous by faith shall live." Faith is the means by which we come to righteousness. Our problem is often that we excuse ourselves for living at a mediocre level.

A boy came home from school and asked his dad for an interpretation of the term "ethics." The father said, "Well, son, I work at the hardware store; now suppose a man comes in and makes a purchase amounting to ten dollars. I hand him the package and he hands me a nice crisp ten-dollar bill. I thank him and turn to put it in the cash register and discover that I have not one but two crisp ten-dollar bills. Now ethics is, do I put one in my pocket and say nothing about it, or do I put it in the drawer and split it with my boss?"

As disciples we come to the Bible with our minds already made up to obey it.

Jesus pronounces a blessing on those who both hear and do his word. In John 8:12 Jesus said, "Whoever follows me will have the light of life and will never walk in the darkness." True faith is a matter of life, not mental assent. Faith is volitional, trust-in-action, a living identification with that which we believe. So, having committed our lives to Christ we read his Word to see what he is asking of us.

The word of the Scriptures is timeless because of its personal and historical nature. It is a personal disclosure of God in Christ. It is authenticated by the actual life experience of millions in the stream of history. No other source can be found for such a personal knowledge of God authenticated in actual human experience. Here is the disclosure of God himself, and the fellowship by which a godly life can be lived. We move to the Word, and in it to Christ, and in Christ to God. We truly know God, whom no man has seen, as a consequence of our faith in Christ. The process of maturing as Christians is to discern Christ's life-style, and thereby participate in Christlike conduct. By following him one can live by the will of God.

As disciples we want our lives conformed to the will of God. Both our minds and our consciences need to be educated by his word. In fact, the conscience is like a computer; it can be programmed! If our commitment to Christ is deep enough, we will reprogram our consciences by the Scriptures. This is a delicate operation and must be done in a prayerful and honest spirit. It is God's word which is the final authority, not man's conscience.

As disciples we discover that the knowledge of God's will comes in proportion to our involvement in it.

We are building a life, and are building upon the solid rock of his truth, not upon the shifting sands of man's speculations. While we are in constant search of the right understanding and application of the knowledge of God, we are no longer in search for God; we've met him in Jesus Christ. Furthermore, the practice of God's will is clear in the life of Christ himself. He is our norm as we understand him in the Scriptures. This is more than an ideal; this is an actual personal pattern. Paul writes that we share with Christ through his Spirit "so that the righteous demands of the Law might be fully satisfied in us who live according to the Spirit, not according to human nature" (Romans 8:4).

In the biblical heritage God is both infinite and personal. He has provided the answer for faith. If God had not already given us some answers, we couldn't ask the right questions. By the information about God in the Scriptures we can ask further questions and find further answers as the Spirit illuminates the Word. The questions a person asks reveal the level of his insight. A man who saw another dragging a chain down the street asked, "Why are you dragging that chain?" The fellow replied, "Did you ever see anyone push one?" Our questions often seem just as shallow when we have only a surface knowledge of the Scriptures. Let us get into the Word, compare scripture with scripture, and let its message take hold of us.

As disciples we recognize that learning comes by doing the things of God.

Jesus put hearing and doing his word together. Just as in skills, so it is in handilng God's Word. I couldn't learn to drive a car or pilot a plane simply by reading a book. No one becomes a heart surgeon simply by reading about it. The way to learn is to participate in doing. Nobody ever becomes skilled in the Word of God just by reading about the Bible or talking about it. There is no substitute for involvement. To be men of the Word we need to spend time in the Word!

There is no substitute for the personal knowledge of God's Word. In a day when time, affluence, and entertainment all take us away from the Word of God, Christ calls us back. The first test of discipleship is whether our basic frame of reference is the Word of God. When this is clear, other issues can be answered in order.

We do not read the Bible alone, for God opens to us its deeper meaning through the circumstances and problems of our lives. Here is where doubts arise and where faith is tried. It is often as expressed by Dostoevski, "I have come to my hosannas through whirlwinds of doubt." But doubt does not come to its answers in and of itself.

If we concede the possibility that we could think our way through our doubts to a meaningful faith, we must also concede that others must have done so before us. We are not alone in our quest. Learning itself is a matter of community, even in scientific research and achievement where one builds upon the discovery or breakthrough of another. Christian faith does not ask us to shut off intellectual inquiry, discovery, and application. On the contrary, it asks us to be honest seekers before the truth of Jesus Christ, open to his Spirit as he leads us to understanding and application of the knowlelge of God and his will.

But too many people in our society haven't read the Bible for themselves. They've heard of someone who has read it—that's about as close as they get! We could at least examine the document with an open mind before we pass judgment on it.

"Faith comes from hearing the message." Reading the document there is no question that it teaches a personal God, a Creator distinct from his creation, an Incarnation in Jesus Christ, a redemption sealed by an actual resurrection of Jesus from the dead, the reality of the baptism with the Holy Spirit, the privilege of forgiveness and the actual experience of a new life in Christ. One may disbelieve, but one cannot disregard the fact that this is the message of the Word. As one studies the Bible, and sees all that it teaches focus in Jesus Christ, he can honestly say with Thomas the disciple, "My Lord, and my God."

As Jesus closes his sermon, his conclusion leaves no doubt about what he is asking. Men then could only marvel and say, "He teaches with authority, not as a lecturer who only parrots information!" Jesus leaves us no escape from decision and no excuse for failure. What we do with his words is the indication of what we do with him.

"Listen, then, if you have ears." (Matthew 13:9.)

Manifesto for Christian Discipleship

Believing that God has confronted man in Jesus Christ, and having committed my life to Christ as Savior and Lord, I accept his call to become an active disciple. Recognizing the rigorous demands of active service which he asks of me, I voluntarily make the following basic commitments as priorities for action.

First, to study and use the Bible daily, to come to the Holy Scriptures with my mind already made up to obey it when I understand it.

Second, to seek above everything else the will of Christ for each situation of life in which I find myself, and his will for aggressive action in his cause.

Third, to honestly face my problems and discipline myself for victory over personal sins of disposition and spirit, as well as overt acts contrary to the principles of righteousness in Christ.

Fourth, to live by nonviolence, and to promote the way of peace, avoiding violence of spirit as well as of act, serving men rather than seeking to rule them.

Fifth, to establish priorities for personal behavior which authenticate my faith-relationship with the risen Christ, so that my freedom and service will be an expression of his presence and lordship in my life.

Sixth, to place the advancement of the Kingdom of Christ ahead of everything material, social, political, and even personal; practicing diligent stewardship with respect to friends, time, and money.

Seventh, to actively witness to others among whom I move in the daily duties of life, calling them to the obedience of faith, and accepting the tension which may arise from this witness as my participation in the Cross of Christ.

It is further understood that this commitment to Jesus Christ as Lord transcends every other commitment and judges every decision I make. It is my prayer that this commitment may lead me to open my life every day to the Holy Spirit for his fullness and for obedience to his sovereign will. With this dedication I join hands with every person of every nation and race who so acknowledges Jesus Christ as Lord and follows him in discipleship.

____

Signature in faith